INTERRUPTED

A Thirty-Day Devotional
for the Busy Mom

Julie Whitley

WESTBOW
PRESS®
A DIVISION OF THOMAS NELSON
& ZONDERVAN

WestBow Press books may be ordered through booksellers or by contacting:

WestBow Press
A Division of Thomas Nelson & Zondervan
1663 Liberty Drive
Bloomington, IN 47403
www.westbowpress.com
844-714-3454

ISBN: 978-1-6642-1168-1 (sc)
ISBN: 978-1-6642-1169-8 (hc)
ISBN: 978-1-6642-1167-4 (e)

Library of Congress Control Number: 2020921948

Print information available on the last page.

WestBow Press rev. date: 11/17/2020

Contents

Preface

Those who know me have described me as a fierce mama bear, unapologetically loyal, independent, dedicated, and strong. I am a wife, mother to four amazing boys, daughter, sister, and friend. With that said, like most moms, I can more than relate to life interruptions. With an undying passion for God's Word and life, I am looking forward to sharing that with you from what others call a "messy" perspective of motherhood. With an ongoing to-do list and never-ending interruptions, I have discovered how God meets us in the chaos. It is my hope that as you read this thirty-day devotional, you will allow God to meet you in life's interruptions.

SECTION 1

Exhaustion

She is fierce and yes has fire in her soul. But sometimes, even she gets exhausted.

—RSN

Coffee. Oh, for the love of coffee. After sleepless nights, early mornings, and endless demands, coffee has become the secret elixir to my supermom strength. Without it, the heroic act of motherhood might just die, or the world, at least as my family knows it, would fall apart.

You may know exactly what I am talking about. Let's face it— we wake up with a daily to-do list that is longer than our children's Christmas lists. We have created a mindset that the to-dos must get done, and we will do whatever it takes. Sounds like an endless competition with ourselves. Each day, our goal is to complete the list, while keeping the kids alive, our marriages whole (if we are married), our friendships solid, and our homes tidy. It's no wonder that every morning, our brains are in a fog. That cup of joe calls us right from our pillows, and our feet hit the floor at high speed, ready to take on the world with our supermom strength.

One of my favorite coffee cups (yes, one; I have many) reads, "Don't talk to me until after I have had my coffee." Deep, I know, but very true. That secret elixir magically gets rid of my brain fog and gives me the first jolt of energy as I start my day. Facing endless demands, day and night, can get exhausting. It's my hope you will enjoy this book daily and fill your cup.

> Come to me, all you who are weary and burdened, and I will give you rest. Take my yoke upon you and learn from me, for I am gentle and humble in heart, and you will find rest for your souls. (Matthew 11:28–29)

1

Work, Work, Work

Stop the glorification of busy.

—UNKNOWN

"You never stop moving," they say. "You never relax," they say. "You need some 'you' time," they say. My response is always the same: "I just have to finish this one last thing."

Before I had my fourth son, I was an administrator for our lead pastor, oversaw several ministries, finished my second year of ministry school, and ran what we call *connect groups* in our home, all while being a wife to a husband in his last year of school and mom to two school-age boys and a toddler. I had some serious supermom skills, driven solely by an ungodly amount of coffee and Jesus. "I can do it; I will do it" was my mantra. I created a system, and it worked—or so I thought.

One evening when we had friends over for dinner, the guys chatted away afterward about some nonsense, and I started clearing the table and putting food away.

My friend said, "Can I help you?"

I responded, "No, it's fine. I've got it."

"Well, you didn't let me help you cook or set the table or serve dinner, and now you are cleaning. When will you be present for a visit? You're always doing something. The mess will be there when we are gone."

Later that night, when I was in bed, her words echoed through my head. *She doesn't understand,* I thought. *I just can't wake up to a messy house.* Was I wrong? I asked my husband if he thought I was rude for cleaning while we had guests.

He responded, "It's not that you were being rude. It's that you never stop. Something always comes between you and spending uninterrupted time with anyone."

That night, I had a lot to think about. How could I balance my work life, ministry, and family and still be a sister, daughter, and friend?

The Bible tells us the following:

> There is a time for everything, and a season for every activity under the heavens: a time to be born and a time to die, a time to plant and a time to uproot, a time to kill and a time to heal, a time to tear down and a time to build, a time to weep and a time to laugh, a time to mourn and a time to dance, a time to scatter stones and a time to gather them, a time to embrace and a time to refrain from embracing, a time to search and a time to give up, a time to keep and a time to throw away, a time to tear and a time to mend, a time to be silent and a time to speak, a time to love and a time to hate, a time for war and a time for peace. (Ecclesiastes 3:1–22)

That seems like common sense, right? Then why do we struggle with this concept of being too busy? The author of Ecclesiastes is showing us there is a season for everything, even day-to-day activities. We must set up boundaries and work within them. A beginning and end time. We need to know when to say no and not overextend ourselves. For example, is washing the endless pile of dishes while cooking dinner and answering every "important" call worth only half hearing about your child's day while he or she tries to express important things? Even though you smile, nod, and say "that's great," there is a part of your child that will feel less important. We need to take the wisdom in this scripture and align our daily lives. Time is the most precious thing we have. It's time to get rid of the clutter so that we are not pumping ourselves with caffeine and trying to push through that to-do list and wearing ourselves out. Then we can be present for what's most important in life.

REFLECTION

Reread Ecclesiastes 3:1–22. What clutter has God asked you to remove from your busy life? What steps can you take to remove it and stay less busy and more present?

PRAYER

Heavenly Father, you have created us moms with super-drive and superstrength, but that does not replace our need for you and your wisdom. We can't do this job without your power and strength. Please speak to our hearts daily and guide us in our time management. Let us never be too busy to hear you speak to our hearts and remind us of what is most important daily. Thank you for the strength you give us to mother the children with whom you have trusted us.

In Jesus's name, we pray. Amen.

2
Helicopter Mom

If I was meant to be controlled, I would have come with a remote.

—Rhode

The room was cold and busy with the hustle and bustle of doctors and nurses in fight-or-flight mode at the delivery of a stillborn. I heard the obstetrician barking orders, nurses scattering, and more teams entering the room. My son's father was crying, and my mom assured me it would be okay. I started to fade in and out of consciousness, but I still mustered enough strength to say, "Where is my baby? Why isn't he crying? Give me my baby."

It was June 7, 2000, the day my first son was born and my mom-instincts kicked in. The delivery was brutal, to say the least, but despite the pain and complications of the delivery, I was concerned with one thing: was my baby okay? It seemed like forever as I waited, unaware of what was happening with my newborn. After three minutes of medical teams resuscitating him, I heard the beautiful sound of the newborn cry. That day changed the course of my life. Killian was put in my arms, and as I looked at his perfect face, I vowed to protect him at all costs.

Between the ages of two and five, we discovered Killian was not just speech impaired but autistic, due to the trauma at birth. We were told he would have a poor quality of life and never graduate from high school. My heart broke as we left the medical facility, and I vowed again to do whatever it took to give him a good and successful life.

You see, we are naturally wired to want to fiercely protect and deeply love our children because we are made in the image of our Creator. Wanting to shelter, protect, and keep them from pain is normal, but when are we helping and when are we hindering? Dr. Pete Enns states, "Good parenting is preparing children to figure things out for themselves as they go along in life, i.e., hovering early on but then looking for ways to stop hovering as soon as possible."[1] There is so much wisdom in that statement, and here is why: if we are made in the image of God, then shouldn't we try to reflect his parenting style? Is he a helicopter parent? Does he control all we do or manipulate us to conform to his wishes? I think not. Instead, he loves us despite our shortcomings and gives us room to grow, while learning from our mistakes. Yup, that's right—learning happens when we make mistakes.

Proverbs 22:6 states, "Train up a child in the way he should go, and when he is old, he will not depart from it." Our job as parents is to train or teach our children. To teach means we need to allow them the room to make mistakes and to learn and grow, yet still be there to show love, forgiveness, and grace. This can be challenging because we naturally want to protect our children from the pains of the world. In trying to protect them from all hurts, pains, and disappointments, society has created a generation of overentitled kids and adults who have no sense of responsibility or ability to take ownership of their wrongs. We have a perfect parent to model; we just have to trust him enough to put his direction into action.

REFLECTION

Remember that God is a God of love, not of control. He has given us free will to love and follow him, but he brings correction to his children and teaches us through our walk with him. How can you stop hovering and start teaching your child/children in this journey of life? Where are

---

[1] Pete Enns, "God Isn't the Great Helicopter Parent in the Sky (At Least That's What the Bible Says)," Pete Enns, July 2013, https://peteenns.com/god-isnt-a-helicopter-parent.

you struggling to let go? Ask God to give you wisdom in that area and illuminate how he would have you handle that situation.

PRAYER

Father God, today we ask for your wisdom and strength. You have trusted us with the gift of motherhood. It is all-consuming and, at times, exhausting; the fear of failure or hurt for our children can be overwhelming, but we know you can handle all things. Please give us the wisdom and clarity to see each situation through your eyes. Remind us how to teach and not control so we can honor you in how we parent our children. Thank you for showing us grace and encouragement when we need it. Show us how to do the same for our children. Help us to lead by your example.

In Jesus's name, we pray. Amen.

3

Champion

The most important thing is to try to inspire people so that they can be great in whatever they want to do.

—KOBE BRYANT

Coffee … I need coffee before the game.

I quickly pulled through the drive-through of a local Dunkin' Donuts and ordered a large coffee. *Yes, caffeine.* I got my coffee and shot across the street to the hockey rink. *I have five minutes to spare before we'll be late; I've got this.*

I found parking and jumped out of the car. "Killian, hurry up and get your pads on," I barked from the back of my SUV, tossing the goalie pads on the ground. "You need to be in the locker room in three minutes."

I quickly pulled the stroller from the car and placed my new baby, Ethan, in it. I strapped him in and covered him with a blanket to keep him warm; I was racing the clock. I turned to finish getting Killian ready, reached into the car, grabbed my coffee, shut the door with my foot, and gave Killian a nudge to run. Coffee one in hand, stroller in the other, we ran across the parking lot. With coffee spilled everywhere, we made it to the locker room just in time.

That night was the biggest night of Killian's little life. His team had gone to the championship and were facing an undefeated team. This was Killian's second year as a goalie, and he was nervous. No matter how I tried to encourage him, he would make himself sick. Killian, like many autistic kids, struggled socially, academically, and emotionally. He was shy and reserved and very timid. His coach, however, had a gift for coaching. Coach Nelson would inspire and encourage the team before and after every game. He believed in them wholeheartedly and got them to believe in themselves. Missing a locker room meeting was out of the question.

I found a spot to stand to cheer on my son. I was in awe as I watched those boys play their hearts out. My son made save after save, and the crowd went wild. The energy was high, and we cheered (well, okay—screamed) from the side of the deck, watching them.

The other team was good, but Killian's team was prepared, and preparation paid off. That night they took home the championship, and Killian was ranked the best goalie in his division—all because someone (not just me) believed in him and didn't give up on him. Galatians 6:9 states, "Let us not become weary in doing good, for at the proper time we will reap a harvest if we do not give up."

That night changed my son's life forever, and it wasn't just because he won the championship; it was because someone poured into him. Yes, I was faithful in getting him to each practice, pushing through my own exhaustion and freezing in twenty-degree weather, running on coffee and no sleep, so he could do what he loved. Even though he didn't have all the skills, someone else took my son under his wing and developed him. That season, he grew in confidence, as a player and a person as a whole.

It's so easy to get weary doing all we do for our children. When we push through, however, we can experience joy in their victories. Sometimes as moms, we need to take a step back and look into our situation from a new angle. Our kids may be too young to express their gratitude or just don't care to. Don't get weary; keep doing what is good, and you will reap a harvest. You will get to see the champion rise from your baby if you don't give up.

REFLECTION

Do you feel like you're running on fumes? Like what you're doing for your kids doesn't matter? Reread Galatians 6:9, and let that be a reminder to persevere, even when you are weary, so that you can see your victory.

PRAYER

Father God, we thank you for your faithful, relentless love for us. Please help us to show the same for our children. Help us to not get weary in our day-to-day grind as moms. If we do, remind us to rest in you so we don't give up. Speak to our hearts daily, and give us a promise that only could come from you to strengthen us in these times.

In Jesus's name, amen.

4

The Power of Laughter

Laugh until your belly hurts and then just a little bit more.

—UNKNOWN

While reading our evening Bible story, my third son, Spencer, asked, "Mom, what's a plague?" At age nine, he was seeking wisdom daily.

Ethan, my now-twelve-year-old, was at the age where he knew everything and was annoyed easily, so he had begun to explain what plagues are, when Johnny, the youngest. interrupted. "Wait ... wait ... wait. What's a slave?" And the rabbit trail began.

"Okay, boys, *focus*," I said. "John, slaves are when people used to keep people like pets and make them do all their hard work for no money. They were treated badly. Spencer, listen to the rest of the Bible story, and you will find out." I continued to read.

John said, "Well, that's not nice. Pharaoh is not nice."

"Okay, boys, enough. Listen."

Every night, the routine was the same. We'd read a story from the Bible, discuss it, pray, and then go to bed. It might sound all spiritual and nice, but most nights didn't look so "spiritual." They looked more like, "Boys, get your drinks. Did you pee? Stop hitting your brother! If you run through my house again ... didn't I tell you to stop screaming? Have you all lost your minds? Get in your room so I can read ... *now*!"

I swear kids have a bedtime sensor that goes off and gives them a second charge just in time to make us crazy. Let's be real, moms— after a long day of work, we are exhausted and just want to get to bed ourselves, so bedtime routines won't always be perfect. But it's important that we have them. On this particular night—one of *those* nights—we were reading about Pharaoh and the Israelites. My boys are very—for lack of a better word—*passionate* about people being bullied or wronged, so this was interesting. We read about the plagues and how the Israelites were free and then set up camp by the sea: "As Pharaoh approached, the Israelites looked up, and there were the Egyptians, marching after them. They were terrified and cried out to the Lord" (Exodus 14:10).

Ethan, in disbelief, mumbled, "What a butt cheek."

Spencer chimed in, frustrated, "Mommy, he's a liar. Why is he going after them?"

John, feeding off Ethan, yelled, "He's a butt cheek on a stick!"

And the room erupted in uncontrollable laughter. I glanced over at my husband for some reinforcement, and he was laughing just as hard.

I couldn't believe what I was seeing and started to laugh myself. "Okay, guys, okay. Let's see what God can do."

I finished the story. We went to bed that night with full hearts.

My husband looked over at me and said, "We don't all laugh together like that often. I had to embrace that moment because we won't get these years back." He was right. It might not have been the time for the inappropriate comment that my five-year-old decided to shout, but his frustration was real, and everyone laughed because my little tiny man has a mighty big mouth. The laughter brought healing to their hearts and brought joy to my husband and me.

God also revealed to me the state of their hearts, the passion they have to be men of their words (not liars), and their desire to please God and honor his Word. I was grateful for that moment. It was a great reminder that laughter is truly medicine for the soul.

REFLECTION

Take a minute to reflect on Proverbs 17:22— "A joyful heart is good medicine, but a crushed spirit dries up bones."

My pastor and mentor used to say to me, "We don't live by feeling; we live by faith. Having joy is a choice." He was right. We don't always feel like laughing, but we have the choice to surrender our hearts to God in worship, finding peace and joy.

PRAYER

Daddy in heaven, thank you for always being present in our lives. Please help us to remember you're always in every situation, especially the dark ones. Help us to choose joy over fear, sorrow, depression, or frustration. Life has its challenges, but nothing is too great for you. Remind us to have a heart of worship, like David, and fill us with your joy so we can laugh and have peace, even in the storms of life.

In Jesus's name, we pray. Amen.

5

Superstrength

Coffee (n): survival juice

—UNKNOWN

"Boys, stop roughhousing."

"We're not; we're playing Spider-Man."

That sentence told me someone would get hurt. I had two options: I could walk into the room, where I most likely would see one of the boys in midair, about to land on the other to get him with a web shooter, or I could wait.

The ear-piercing scream of a crying child echoed through the house. The older boys were frantically fumbling over each other, trying to get out of the room to plead their case to me. Meanwhile, the youngest was holding his head and crying.

I didn't even look up from my cup of coffee. I just nodded my head, pointed my finger, and said, "*Go!* I told you, no roughhousing." While I checked John's head, I asked, "Why do you keep playing so rough?"

He looked up at me and said, "Mom, I just want to be Spider-Man!"

Whether superheroes are protecting the night when the signal calls, swinging from buildings, shooting webs, leaping tall buildings in single bound, or flying high in a suit of armor, superheroes have made a mark on all, young and old. There is something to be said for humans with superstrength (mutants, if you will). We are drawn to them; their power, strength, and virtue captivates us. But it's not the strength that makes them super, or we would not have equally-as-cool villains. Yes, villains have cool superpowers too, but who wants the villain to win? No one.

What makes most children and adults love heroes is their relatability and their character—what they choose to do with their superpower: save the world. I've often wished I could be a female version of Iron Man. He is super strong, smart, efficient, organized, and a great leader. The man behind the armor is just about bulletproof. I'm inspired by his drive and ability to execute all tasks while inspiring others to be great.

But most days, I feel like Elastigirl, the mother with the superpower of flexibility in *The Incredibles*. As the clock hits 5:45 a.m., I jump out of bed and start the mad dash through the house, making the crew breakfast, waking up the kids, swallowing coffee, packing snacks, handing bags to kids, and cleaning up before pushing them out the door to wait at the bus stop. It is only 7:45, and I am already charged and marking my next target that's going down.

Sometimes, my kids joke and say, "Mom, you remind us of Elastigirl. We don't even see your hand coming when you hit us in the back of the head to pay attention."

Elastigirl—yup, she is pretty incredible, but man, I would love to *not* be incredibly tired. Motherhood is probably the most exhausting job in the world. If we want to do it well, it's clear that we need superstrength.

> I am not saying this because I am in need, for I have learned to be content whatever the circumstances. I know what it is to be in need, and I know what it is to have plenty. I have learned the secret of being content in any and every situation, whether well fed or hungry, whether living in plenty or in want. I can do all this through him who gives me strength. (Philippians 4:11–13)

What the apostle Paul is trying to tell us in the above scripture is that in great times and hard times, we need to have a heart of surrender to God and draw our strength from his Word and his promises, not from resources around us that will come and go. The secret elixir (double-shot espresso with steamed milk) won't sustain us or transform us to supermoms with superstrength on its own.

Don't feel defeated when you're running on fumes, with three hours of sleep and a household to keep together. We need to drink from a deeper cup and draw our strength from above. It is then our superstrength comes out because the God in us supplies all our needs, and that includes strength.

REFLECTION

Have you ever wanted to harness the power of a superhero? What character traits draw you to the superhero? Do you possess some of those traits? Read Philippians 4:13 again, and reflect on what it would look like for you to surrender all to God, including time.

PRAYER

Heavenly Father, today, we ask you to illuminate our path and day. Please show us where we need to focus our time and energy, so we achieve all we need to do for our families and work life. Fill us with your presence and strength so that we find that same contentment as apostle Paul in all situations. Help us to feel accomplished in what we do, and, most importantly, thank you for the supernatural strength you give us daily. In Jesus's name, we pray. Amen.

6

Perfect ... Just Perfect

*There is no way to be a perfect mother, but
a million ways to be a good one.*

—UNKNOWN

Wake up, wipe the sleep from my eyes, and head to the kitchen to make coffee. Back to my room to get ready for the day, still half asleep. The smell of caffeine brewing hits my soul, and I am suddenly awake. It's 6:00 a.m., time to wake Ethan for school, make breakfast, then wake Spencer (because God forbid they wake up at the same time—that's a war in the bathroom), put snacks in bags, feed the children, hand out meds, all while shouting, "Boys, stay on task. Stop playing around. We need to get to the bus stop."

Then make my cup of coffee, wash dishes, toss in a load of laundry, clean cat box, take out the trash or recycling, grab my coffee and middle child, and head out the door to the bus stop. While at the bus stop, we hold hands with the neighborhood kids and say a morning prayer before heading off to school.

Seems like a normal day, except this day was one of the many I replay in my head, trying to determine how the morning could have been less hectic. The kids' clothes were laid out the night before, bags were lined up by the door, snacks were on the island, and I just needed to get to the book bags, yet every morning seemed like a whirlwind of crazy. It's even worse when I don't have enough quiet time to spend with God first.

I would love to say I start every day, one-on-one with the Lord, but that's just not true. After long nights of no sleep, I am lucky to pull myself out of bed by six o'clock and get the day going at all. Yet I can't help but feel a sense of failure when I don't read my Word first thing (even if it happens later in the day or evening). I start to question all things: "Why am I so grumpy? Why did I snap at the boys so much? I didn't get to spend quiet time with the Lord; how are my kids going to know the importance of a relationship with God if they don't see me doing it? I bet the moms on the leadership teams don't have this problem." The list of self-doubt goes on. But news flash—if other moms have more than one kid, their homes are probably just as crazy as mine in the morning.

We need to stop trying to be perfect moms; stop comparing ourselves to others and give ourselves some grace. We also need to acknowledge that we are flawed and not perfect. We have weaknesses and shortcomings.

> But he said to me, "My grace is sufficient for you, for my power is made perfect in weakness." Therefore, I will boast all the more gladly about my weaknesses, so that Christ's power may rest on me. (2 Corinthians 12:9)

When we take those weaknesses and bring them to the Lord, his power is made perfect in our weakness. That means his supernatural strength will show in our time of need. Jesus *is* our *super-suit*. He is the source of our strength. He is fully aware of our shortcomings and offers us his grace so we can continue to grow in love and grace.

We need to look at ourselves, using the same lens through which our Lord sees us. We would not expect our children to carry such a heavy burden, so why model that? That shows them there is no need for a God if we can handle life on our own, right? If we only want them to do their best, not be perfect, then the same should hold true for us moms. We can't be perfect, but we can be our best, and our best is perfect for them.

REFLECTION

Are you struggling with being perfect? Write down where you feel you're falling short and ask the Lord to illuminate if you are trying to do things on your own or in his strength. Reflect on 2 Corinthians 12:9. What is the Lord speaking to you?

PRAYER

Lord, thank you for your grace and your love. As we go through the day, help us to tap into your strength, and when we fall short, help us to accept it and move forward with grace and peace. Please help us to see we will never be perfect moms, but with your help, we are great moms. Help us to continue to operate in your strength, in your grace, with wisdom you provide.

In Jesus's name, we pray. Amen.

SECTION 2

Mom Guilt

*There will be so many days where you feel
like you've failed. But in the eyes, heart, and
mind of your child, you are super mom.*

—STEPHANIE PRECOURT

As a teenager, I swore up and down I would never be like my mother. I would be a better mother—or so I thought. Shortly after my first son was born, I became a single mom. I moved into the studio section of my parents' home and braved this thing called motherhood at age twenty. Killian was the most precious gift, yet I found myself confused, unsure, and scared. I called my mom multiple times a day, crying with frustration and feelings of failure. "The baby won't stop crying. He won't sleep. I can't sleep. Make him stop. *Take this baby!*" So much for being a better mom.

According to *Webster's Dictionary*, *mom guilt* is "the feeling of guilt, doubt, anxiousness, or uncertainty experienced by mothers when they worry, they're failing or falling short of expectations in some way." Who would have thought that having a child would create such a feeling of inadequacy and failure? Yet it does. From the time our children are born, we dread going back to work; we dread leaving them with a sitter to go out on a date night; we dread deciding whether to breastfeed or bottle-feed; we even dread explaining our positions on feeding them commercial baby food or homemade food—the list continues as they grow. We put unnecessary pressure on ourselves to be supermoms. But for who? For us, for our children, or for others to see? That is certainly not what God had in mind when he gave us the gift of motherhood, but motherhood is not just a gift from God; it's a journey of love and grace—an opportunity to share life, love, laughter, and the light of the Lord with the little humans he has entrusted to us.

> A little boy forgot his lines in a Sunday school presentation. His mother was in the front row to prompt him. She gestured and formed the words silently with her lips, but it did not help. Her son's memory was blank. Finally, she leaned forward and whispered the cue, "I am the light of the world." The child beamed and with great feeling and a loud clear voice said, "My mother is the light of the world."[2]

That little boy was reassured by his mom and, with bold confidence, he expressed his lines. Although he said his line incorrectly, the fact that his mom was there when he needed her gave him strength and confidence to get through that scary moment. She was his hero, and she was simply there. Remember moms: we don't have to be perfect, just present and available.

---

[2] "My Mother: The Light of The World," Bible.org, August 1989, http://bible.org/illustration/my-mother-light-world.

7

The Woman in the Mirror

*My mother taught me that true beauty comes
from within and that validation and self-
worth must also come from within.*

—ASHLEY GRAHAM

It was 2:00 a.m., and I had not slept a wink. With a heavy heart and a broken spirit, I sat in bed, reflecting on all that I had lost in life—from dreams to an athletic body. I hated the women I saw in the mirror. The sound of Spencer crying brought me back to reality. Quickly, I jumped out of bed to get him from his crib. It was time for his usual feeding. Not long after sitting down to nurse him, I got lost in my thoughts again. Tears streamed down my face. I tried to get a grip by looking into Spencer's little eyes. "I love you so much, yet I hate myself. How is this possible? Is this all I have become?"

I'll never forget that night—the night I realized motherhood had cost me everything. I wanted to be the "perfect" mom yet, nothing was ever enough.

Is this all I have become? I thought. I wondered how many others could relate to that ugly reality.

See, in my mission to be the perfect mom (not making the same mistakes my mom made), I gave my kids *all* of me. I was there for every moment of every day, giving them everything, at every demand—God forbid, I wasn't available when they called. What I didn't realize was that being *always* available to them meant I said no to myself. Years later, after child number three, I felt the pain of failure and disgust. I looked in the mirror and hated who I saw. I felt unattractive and uncomfortable in my skin. I didn't own any cute clothes, and the sex appeal I once had was gone. That meant I no longer felt attractive for my husband. That led to a whole other battery of insecurities. Romans 12:2 says, "Do not conform to the pattern of this world but be transformed by the renewing of your mind. Then you will be able to test and approve what God's will is—his good, pleasing and perfect will."

The first problem was my "stinking thinking." I hated what I allowed myself to become, but only I could change that. I had to change my perspective. I needed to get on my face before the Lord and ask him to renew my mind and to help me to love myself where I was. I needed to not conform my thought patterns to what society deemed as attractive or sexy. I needed to believe that the vows my husband and I made before God were stronger than my insecurities. All that started with the renewing of my mind.

I knew it wasn't God's will that I was depressed and fearful of a broken marriage. That evening, I cried out to God to help me in this desperate place—to help me love myself the way he saw me and to give me the ability to be healthy and not chase vanity. That evening ended with me ordering a workout program called P90X and a commitment before God and my baby that I would reclaim my health, my self-esteem, and my peace of mind. And the journey began.

REFLECTION

Reflect on Romans 12:2. Depression has no place in our lives; fear has no place, and neither does inadequacy or shame. Make time to set those things at the feet of our Savior, and be transformed by the renewing of your mind.

JULIE WHITLEY

PRAYER

Heavenly Father, thank you for loving us in our broken places. Today, I ask you to search our hearts. Bring forth the insecurities, pains, and things that would cause us to fall prey to depression. Lord, I ask that you renew our minds, and strengthen us in these moments. May your Word breathe life into our bones and fire in our hearts, that we may be strengthened in these dark areas.

In Jesus's name, we pray. Amen.

8

Is This It?

Appreciate where you are in your journey, even if it's not where you want to be. Every season serves a purpose.

—UNKNOWN

"I am going to be a machinist."

"I want to be Spider-Man."

"I want to be a contractor … and build houses for the poor around the world."

"Mom, I don't know what I want to be."

I quickly responded to that final comment. "That's okay, bud. You have plenty of time to figure it out. You can be whatever you want, as long as you are happy and educated."

It was one of those nights when the boys and I talked about our future and our dreams. Killian, my eldest, followed his passion and decided he wanted to become a machinist. My youngest wanted to be Spider-Man; and Ethan wanted to build homes on the mission field. But the one that hit me the hardest was from my nine-year-old, Spencer, when he said, "I don't know what I want to be."

Truth is, do we ever know? When I was Spencer's age, I wanted to be a writer, a hairdresser, a police officer, a physiatrist, and a model. That list stayed fairly consistent right through high school, except *police officer* turned into *criminal profiler*. I started writing more in high school and saving my work. I modeled during my junior year, until my mom pulled me out—first dream crushed. When I graduated from high school, I went to school to become a profiler. Shortly after my second semester in college, I found out I was pregnant with my first son. I watched my dream begin to fade as I weighed the risk associated with being a profiler. Was I willing to risk being hunted by the very people I was trying to put behind bars? Was I willing to risk leaving my son for days or weeks to close a case? Not a chance.

Not willing to take the obvious risk of being a profiler and mother, I changed careers and went to school to be a hairdresser. Over the years, I became a jack of all trades, master of none. I would be lying if I said I never thought where my life would be if I had stuck with profiling or had taken the job offer as a hairdresser for models and actresses. Where would I be if I had stayed in modeling?

But focusing on my past "losses" did nothing but depress me, taking me away from the present. I wanted to be a mom! And being a mom means sacrifices. Yes! Even my big career plans were sacrificed to be the mom I wanted to be. I would cry many nights, asking myself, "Is this it? I will cook, clean, and be underappreciated the rest of my life—that's what I signed up for?"

One Sunday at church, a woman I respect came up to me and said, "You were on my heart. I prayed for you, and God wants you to know you're in a season. Don't be discouraged; enjoy the season."

At that time, I just nodded and smiled, thinking, *When will it be over?*

But man, was she right. So much happens in the first five years of our kids' lives, and although it seems like forever, it's not. When they are twelve or twenty, we will wonder where the time went. The Bible says, "Let us not become weary in doing good, for at the proper time we will reap a harvest if we do not give up" (Galatians 6:9).

Let's not get weary doing what God has put before us. That will only lead to stinking thinking—depression and the mindset that we are missing out, that there is something better than what we have. But what would be the sacrifice for that "better"? Our children? How many mothers with successful careers would have loved to be there for their children's first step or laugh or to have comforted them when they were sick or scared? Think about that—it's a season. Embrace the season while preparing for the future. We don't need to give up on the dreams in our hearts. We just need to wait for the right season, and then those doors will open.

REFLECTION

Are you growing weary? Feeling overworked and undervalued? God sees all we do. He knows the desires of our hearts. Don't let the enemy steal your joy or distract you from the call to motherhood. Reflect on Galatians 6:9, and apply it to yourself. Write down that dream or goal that you want to accomplish—that thing that has you distracted or feeling like you're missing out. Remember: God knows, so bring it to him in prayer, ask for direction to accomplish that desire, and embrace your season, while planning for your future.

PRAYER

Heavenly Father, you know our hearts, our dreams, and the visions you gave to us. We pray that you keep those things burning in our hearts when we grow weary. Help us to reflect on the promise of your Word, and renew our strength. Help us to manage our time wisely, while we plan for new seasons, yet still enjoy the season we are in. Thank you for giving us the opportunity to be mothers. Most importantly, thank you for guiding, protecting, and loving us and for showing us the example we are to be for our children.

In Jesus's name, we pray. Amen.

9

We Are Incredible

We do everything besides leap tall buildings in a single bound. We are superheroes without capes.

—DEBBIE BURGIN

My kids loves all things superheroes. We named our dog Dash after Mr. Incredible's son. One evening, while watching *Incredibles 2*, the boys laughed hysterically. "Look, Mom! It's Dad!" they shouted.

I glanced at the TV just in time to see Mr. Incredible's rant after spending a few days playing Mr. Mom while his wife was away: "Because I'm formulating, okay! I'm taking in information! I'm processing! I'm doing the math. I'm fixing the boyfriend and keeping the baby from turning into a flaming monster! How do I do it? By rolling with the punches, baby! Because I'm Mr. Incredible! Not 'Mr. So-So' or 'Mr. Mediocre Guy'! Mr. Incredible!"

The kids were laughing so hard, and I let out a giggle too. There was some element of truth to that scene. Mr. Incredible had not slept in days. He had not shaved or showered, and he looked like a hot mess. What he had thought would be "a piece of cake" turned out to be a lot different than he had expected. The "mom responsibilities" were not as easy as they looked.

There is a lesson in the scene, but it's not, *don't leave your kids home with Dad because they can't handle it*. It's a message of balance—mental, physical, and spiritual balance.

For while bodily training is of some value, godliness is of value in every way, as it holds promise for the present life and also for the life to come. (1 Timothy 4:8)

Mr. Incredible was physically strong but not mentally strong. He was trying to navigate uncharted grounds on an empty tank. Unfortunately, at times, we do the same.

No matter how prepared we are, how strong we are, how organized we are, if we try to do life without balance, we will fail. We are not wired to work on our own strength. The burden is far too great. This is why the Bible talks about the importance of our "resting in God," being "alone with God," and "finding time of solitude." Jesus did this himself, and we need to follow that example, making our mental and spiritual health a priority daily. Godly living does not happen by accident; it is intentional and takes discipline. I don't know about you, but on the days that I don't have alone time with God, I feel overwhelmed and get frazzled a lot easier.

There have been many days when I've decided to conquer the world on my own and have failed. It is near impossible to sustain our best, emotionally and mentally, if we are drained spiritually. It will catch up to us, and when it does, we will look like Mr. Incredible did in the scene mentioned above.

Don't allow the business of life to distract you from spending quality time with our Creator. If you can't spend the first part of your morning in his presence and the Word, bring a Bible or devotion to work with you. (There are many options on smartphones nowadays.) Read on your lunch break or when you get home at night. It is so important to spend that time alone with God so he can fill us, direct us, and sustain us. After all, he made us moms pretty incredible.

REFLECTION

Have you been short-fused lately, or have you felt like you're losing your mind? When was the last time you spent quiet time with the Lord (not bullet prayers or a quick read)? Remember what 1 Timothy 4:8 says: "For while bodily training is of some value, godliness is of value in every way, as it holds promise for the present life and also for the life to come."

We can't have godliness without time spent with him. Make that time a priority and schedule it into your day.

PRAYER

Heavenly Father, we thank you for our incredible strength to get through each day like superheroes. Thank you for always showing up, even when we don't deserve it. Lord, help us to find balance in a world of chaos. Place a burning desire in our hearts for your Word, and give us a thirst that can be quenched only by you. Lord, as we seek you daily, give us wisdom, and help us to walk in your peace when the challenges of motherhood become unbearable.

In Jesus's name, we pray. Amen.

10

Stranger

Emotionally: I'm done.
Mentally: I'm drained.
Spiritually: I'm dead.
Physically: I smile.

—UNKNOWN

I see you ...
At a distance, the fire in your eyes, the laughter in
your heart.
I see you ...
Full of life and passion, a visionary ready to conquer
the world to achieve your dreams.
I see you ...
At a distance, staring back through the reflection of
my shattered dreams.
I see you ...
So far out of reach; I knew you once.
That girl in the mirror.

While navigating different seasons of life, I have written many
poems—poems of shattered dreams, lost hope, and the pain of
depression. As I looked back on them, I realized they all had one
thing in common: the word *stranger*. With that realization, the poem
above was birthed.

Maybe you have been in that place where you feel like you are two different people; maybe you're there now. The person you wanted to be is lost in the reality of obstacles that life has tossed at you. Maybe you have never been there but know someone who feels that way. The good news is, we don't need to stay there. Jesus is an overcomer; he conquered the grave. We were made in his image. Therefore, we are also overcomers. His plan for us is not to sit in darkness, feeling defeated, alone, lost, and hopeless. We were made to fulfill the purpose and plan for which he placed us here. The passion that burned inside us was given to us by him, but how we handle the obstacles in life is our choice.

We can fan that fire, or we can give up.

I chose to fan the fire. It was not always easy, but the Bible says for us to ask God and believe. That means ask, and know that he is working in our situations, even if we don't see it.

> But when you ask, you must believe and not doubt, because the one who doubts is like a wave of the sea, blown and tossed by the wind. That person should not expect to receive anything from the Lord. Such a person is double-minded and unstable in all they do. (James 1:6–8)

We need to believe in the same way a young child believes in the myth of Santa or even how children believe in Jesus. If you tell a child that Jesus can do something, they won't question you. They'll just say, "OK! Jesus will do it!" That's the kind of unwavering faith we need to have. If we ask and doubt, we are double-minded. We feel torn; we give the enemy a foothold so he can play with our emotions, and shortly, we fall prey to his tactics—we convince ourselves that we somehow have missed all God had for us in life.

We stare in the mirror at a stranger, wondering where the woman we knew went. No matter if you were or are in this place—hit your knees and ask God to fan the fire he placed in your heart. With unwavering faith, say goodbye to the stranger.

Reflection

Do you feel like you are staring at a stranger in the mirror? Have you asked God to fan the flame he placed in you? Reflect on James 1:6–9, and remind yourself to go to God with unwavering faith.

Prayer

Heavenly Father, we ask you to open doors and opportunity for our lives. We understand that you know what is best for us, and we trust you completely. But today, we ask for you to ignite the flame in our hearts for the passion you gave us. Give us direction, wisdom, and the ability to balance life as we walk this new path, following your direction.

In Jesus's name, we pray. Amen.

11

Hypoxia

"Oh ... hypoxia. When you don't have enough oxygen, things seem really silly. Things get sillier and sillier, and then you die."

—THE INCREDIBLES

I love to travel, probably because I was raised in a military home and had the privilege (although I didn't think that when I was young) of traveling across the United States and seeing the beauty in other countries.

The above quote from *The Incredibles* is in a scene on an airplane. The villain, Evelyn, was trying to get away from the Incredibles, but Elastigirl boarded the plane to stop her. The scene shows Evelyn, driving the plane like a getaway car—climbing at high speed and high altitude while wearing an oxygen mask. The hero, Elastigirl, tries to navigate the erratic plane to stop Evelyn, but she's not wearing an oxygen mask. She almost makes it to the villain when she begins to act silly, and the villain explains, "Oh ... hypoxia. When you don't have enough oxygen, things seem really silly. Things get sillier and sillier, and then you die."

Elastigirl exclaims, "I don't want to die."

That is a sobering thought. She had no mask, and she was trying to save the world at the cost of her own life. Although that is a scene in a movie, it holds an element of truth. When you travel on a plane, the crew gives instructions on how to escape the plane safely in an emergency. The crew also instructs you to place your oxygen mask on your face prior to helping others, including your own children. Some people don't understand this procedure, but it's simple: how can you help a panicking child if you pass out or die in the process?

Every day, we become pilots, carefully flying through life. We make breakfast, do the laundry, kiss the boo-boos, and tend to the husband, the house, the friends, and, for some, the elderly parents. But are we putting on our masks first? Where are we drawing our strength? It is so important to make sure that we are caring for ourselves so that we can continue to care for others. Making ourselves a priority is not selfish—just the opposite. It is ensuring we are giving the best form of us to others. Taking time for ourselves ensures that we are in the right frame of mind emotionally and spiritually, as well as physically. I'm not suggesting spending the entire day, while kids are in school or daycare, pampering yourself and then trying to cram a day's worth of duties into a couple of hours before kids get home. I'm saying to find that balance of taking an hour or so for yourself—time when you can exercise, go for a walk, have coffee with a friend, or just spend quiet time with the Lord, allowing him to love you. Take uninterrupted time—so you can be at your best. God created us with the deep desire to love and care for our families, but we can't do that when we're on empty—without oxygen. We need to allow God to breathe into our souls daily. He is our oxygen mask. He fills our cups, and he renews our minds so we can continue to pour into others daily.

> The Lord will guide you continually, giving you water when you are dry and restoring your strength. You will be like a well-watered garden, like an ever-flowing spring. (Isaiah 58:11)

REFLECTION

Do you struggle with making time for yourself? Think about hypoxia; what good are you to your family if you are physically burned out and emotionally and spiritually dead? I challenge you to reflect on Isaiah

58:11. It says, "You will be like a well-watered garden." A well-watered garden produces great fruit. It says you will "be like an ever-flowing spring"; that means you will have plenty to pour out. But in order to do that, you need to care for yourself first, and make time to allow God to love you, restoring your strength during your quiet time.

PRAYER

Father God, thank you for your deep and unconditional love. Thank you for restoring us when we are weak and weary so that we can continue to pour into others. Today, we pray that as life gets busy, you give us a sign to remember to place our masks on first. Quicken our spirits to remind us to draw near to you and rest in your presence daily.

In Jesus's name, we pray. Amen.

12

Life Interrupted

We must be ready to allow ourselves to be interrupted by God.
—DIETRICH BONHOEFFER

Like most high school seniors, I had big plans for after graduation. The prospect of going out and making my mark in the real world gave me a sense of both power and excitement. High school was the training ground for learning who I was, what I was made of, and how I was going to make a difference in this world.

I grew up watching my mom and dad work hard and struggle to give us a good life. Raising three kids while in school and working full time is no easy feat, but my mom made it look natural. However, she revealed the overwhelming burdens of life late at night, when her sobs of frustration would echo through the walls of our bathroom. My mom was driven, strong, self-motivated, and smart. I hated hearing her cry, and I definitely did not want to experience the burdens that she felt. So when she gave me advice, I would hide it in my heart.

She often stressed that education was the single most important thing in life. She said, "Julie, I don't care if you are a doughnut maker as long as you're an educated one. The difference between being good at something and excellent at it is the amount of work you put in to learning your trade. No matter what you choose to be in life, choose to be excellent at it. Good is not good enough."

Those words propelled me to always strive for greatness. After graduation, my friends and I took different paths. I was supposed to

JULIE WHITLEY

join one of my best friends in the air force while pursuing my studies as a criminal profiler. But that spring, right before recruitment, I found out I was pregnant. I cried and told my mom, "My life is over." All my dreams had come to a screeching halt, and life, as I knew it, was interrupted. I now had to think of what would be best for the baby inside me and, most importantly, what kind of mother I wanted to be.

That night was one of the most important nights of my life—the night I found out I would be a mom, the night my dreams died in front of me, and the night I sacrificed all I had in mind for love. After that, there were many nights when I saw my "super-successful" friends, and I later cried in bed, wondering if my life would have been different if I had taken a different path. Tears of pain and failure would stream down my face as I measured myself against others' success. But the Word states, "Many are the plans in the mind of a man, but it is the purpose of the Lord that will stand" (Proverbs 19:21 ESV).

For my entire life, I have wanted to make a difference. I measured my worth and success in a job title, but that was *my* big plan, not God's. He did not want me to plant my identity in a corporate job title. He wanted me to find my worth in him. I needed to trust in his plans and not mine. When I changed my perspective, I realized that my margin of impact and influence was greater than my mind could have imagined. The difference I make starts in my home with my children, husband, family, and friends. The promise God gave me was to teach others about his goodness, love, and mercy in a tangible way. My reach is endless.

Go to the world and make disciples. (Matthew 28:19)

High school was my training ground in my early years. Motherhood was the training ground that pushed me to my knees, teaching me to rely completely on God to guide me daily. Life would be different for me if I had taken a different path. But that interruption caused me to draw closer to God, pursuing his plans, and that's where I found my purpose—in his plans.

Now, nothing can replace the fire that fills my bones and ignites me with that same excitement, power, and passion that I had when I was young.

REFLECTION

Where did your plans get interrupted? Reflect on Proverbs 19:21. Surrender your plans to God's feet and remind yourself that his purpose for our lives will stand. Ask God how your plans can line up with his purpose, and get ready for the ride.

PRAYER

Heavenly Father, thank you for the ability to dream big, to have passion, and to desire great things in life. Thank you for the gifts we see and the ones we don't yet see. Today, we ask that you reveal to us how our plans can line up with your purpose in our lives. Give us direction so that we are walking in the call you have given us, filling our hearts with passion and purpose.

In Jesus's name, we pray. Amen.

❧

SECTION 3

Pressure of Perfection

Don't try to be perfect. Life isn't; none is. Use mistakes and mishaps as opportunities to grow tolerance and to teach. There is such a thing as happy accidents. And love, love, love and listen, listen, listen.

—TERRI HATCHER

I'll never forget the time I was rushing to put Killian in his car seat early one Saturday morning (six o'clock, to be exact). He was two years old and full of energy. I was an exhausted single mom. After a couple of minutes of battling the toddler to strap him in the car seat, I finally won. We were off to Dunkin' Donuts to get coffee. *Coffee! I need coffee*—that's all my brain could comprehend that morning. I ordered my large hazelnut coffee and a doughnut for the monster in the back. As the lady handed me my order through the window, I heard Killian say, "Hi, you're pretty."

I apologized to the lady and had turned to speak to Killian about his comment when I noticed he no longer had his clothes on. He had removed everything, right down to his underpants. I was mortified.

I wasn't sure what to say, but I apologized again and drove off as fast as I could.

Every time we got in a car, Killian had the need to get naked. I could never keep his clothes on him. No matter where we went, I had to fight him to get dressed in every parking lot, while parents walking by stared at me with disapproval. Why could I never "control" my kid? Why was I always losing my head and looking like a hot mess? I hated going out because I didn't understand why I'd failed to be a "good mom." I could never get my act together like a normal mom.

As I've said, I made it my life mission to be excellent in everything I did because good was not good enough. But the one thing I never seemed to be able to master was motherhood. For some reason, I always missed the mark. The Bible says, "Enthusiasm without knowledge is no good; haste makes mistakes" (Proverbs 19:2 NLT).

Reflecting on that time, I can see what my mom was trying to tell me. Slow down, understand where my autistic child was developmentally, be patient, and be prepared. Although it didn't make sense to me then, it made sense as I got older. I was young and narrow-minded. I moved at one speed to execute the tasks that I felt were important, often making mistakes. Proverbs 19:2 is a good reminder that no matter how passionate we are about something, no matter how long our to-do list is, and no matter how little time we have, we need to slow down. We need to make sure we understand the situation or the moments we are in to avoid making silly mistakes.

When you make mistakes (and you will), give yourself the grace to learn and grow from it. After all, no one is perfect.

13

Revolving Door

Housekeeping is like being caught in a revolving door.
—MARCELENE COX

I have countless memories from my growing-up years of my mother losing her patience when we failed to do our chores correctly. Nothing drove her crazier than the sight of an unclean house. When we failed to do our chores, she would shout, "You call this house clean? It's not; it's picked up. There is a difference between the two. Do your chores."

But the days when Mom spent hours cleaning were the worst. After we also had cleaned for hours and were exhausted, we would hear her yell for us in frustration. We'd run down the stairs and stand before her for questioning. "Who left dishes in the sink?"

The room would remain silent until one of us got the nerve to say, "I don't know."

Then the lecture began: "Oh, so now we have an invisible man living here—the I-don't-know man. He always leaves messes and then magically disappears—and no one knows he did it. He needs to go!"

How I hated that lecture. I didn't understand what the big deal was—then I had kids of my own.

Starting the day with the to-do list running through your head and your super strong coffee elixir in your hand, you plan to conquer the world, one chore at a time. Seems simple, but for some reason, that never gets done. Start the laundry; clean the kitchen; get to the living room, only to find, when that room is done, that the kitchen has been visited by the I-don't-know man, who always leaves dishes on the table and leaves the counters dirty. I couldn't agree more with my mom—that man needs to go! You put laundry in the dryer before you grab the kids and head out to run errands, and then you go back home to start dinner and finish chores, and I am sure there's a bunch more stuff in between—attending to needs, helping with homework, answering phones, defusing fights, and, somewhere in all that, having time to go to the bathroom yourself.

I was raised in a clean home. We all were expected to do chores (the I-don't-know man lived there too). If our chores where not done, we felt the wrath of Mom. I never understood what the big deal was; our house never seemed "dirty." Yet my mom always said, "There is a difference between clean and picked up."

Now, as an adult, I know what she meant, and I have fallen victim to the endless-housework revolving door. I can't image not having what I consider a presentable house—if people where to pop in, my face would fall in embarrassment. But the truth is, what am I sacrificing to achieve this "perfect house"? Time with my children or my husband? My sanity? Is it worth the stress to have a house that is showroom clean (as opposed to lived-in and slightly messy) but with an unhappy family?

If we focus all our time on trying to maintain the perfect house, we will miss out on many more important things. The story of Martha and Mary gave me a huge wake-up call. when I was struggling in this area. Martha had invited Jesus to her home but then was stressed out and distracted by all the preparations needed to be a good host (much as I have done many times). "She came to Jesus and asked, "Lord, don't you care that my sister has left me to do the work by myself? Tell her to help me!"

"Martha, Martha," the Lord answered, "you are worried and upset about many things, but few things are needed—or, indeed, only one. Mary has chosen what is better, and it will not be taken away from her."

Martha was looking for Jesus to be on her side and to say, "Get up and help your sister, lazy. Don't you see she can't rest if she is doing it all?" (At least, that's what I would have wanted him to say if I were Martha.) Instead, the lesson was for Martha. Mary had chosen the right thing. The things around her were not as important as the bigger picture—sitting in God's presence. Mary chose right.

So before you get stuck in the revolving door of housework, and bring down the "wrath of mom" on your children for their lack of help, and become completely exhausted, ask yourself, what is *most* important today? Take time to watch the kids laugh and play, and connect with them, worship together, and get in God's presence. (My youngest loves to worship and swears he will be like Chris Brown from the band Elevation Worship.) Build on those moments. We only have them for a season, so let's get it right, like Mary. The mess will be there later.

REFLECTION

Are you stuck in a revolving door—the trap of endless household responsibilities. Are you feeling the pressure of never having downtime? Are you burned out from the demands you face daily? Reflect on Luke 10:40–42, and ask yourself if you are more Martha or more Mary. Ask God to show you how to do what's right to escape the revolving door.

PRAYER

Father God, thank you for giving us a servant's heart. Thank you for creating us with the desire to make our family happy and to serve friends, family, and, most important, you. We pray today that you reveal to our hearts how to make better choices daily so we are not overwhelmed and overworked. Help us to choose what is right, and give us a fresh perspective to let go of the things that are *not* most important. Help us to rest in your presence and to find peace in the changes we need to make. In Jesus's name, amen.

14

The Bully

Parenting is the easiest thing in the world to have an
opinion about. But the hardest thing in the world to do.

—Matt Walsh

Fourth grade was a rough year for Ethan. He went from being the "quiet Christian boy" to having bad reports (called *think sheets*) sent home almost weekly. Something changed in him that year, and I was not sure what it was. His grades started to slip, his attitude was indifferent, and he was not the same boy I knew. No matter how much I kept on him for his attitude and behavior, nothing seemed to work. I watched as my little boy who loved God and his Word became a stone-cold stranger. Although physically present, he was not there during church or family devotions. I just could not put my finger on the change.

One Sunday evening after church, as I was prepping for the week, Ethan walked up to me with yet another think sheet. This report was different. It shook me at my core. It was a report of Ethan being part of a bullying ring. I would like to say that I handled the situation with grace and that I was level-headed, but the exact opposite was true. As I read the report, I instantly was enraged. I saw red, and my arm stretched toward him across the table and chairs. I grabbed him by the front of his shirt and drew him close to me. I lost it.

Tears of anger and disappointment streamed down my face as I began to scold him. "*How dare you?* Who do you think you are? I didn't raise you like that. Don't you remember your brother's best friend killed himself because of the hateful words of stupid kids being nasty? Do you want to be the reason someone ends their life? I will beat you before allowing that in this house. Do you even know what this kid's life is like at home?" My anger continued to climb, and at this point, I am sure the entire block heard me. "If I ever see or hear—"

I couldn't finish the sentence. I let him walk away. The anger in me was overwhelming, and I needed space to get control. Once I'd calmed down, I called him to the living room. Apparently, I had placed the fear of God in him because my hard son had tears in his eyes.

"Question," I said. "Last year, Leroy was new to the school. You told Leroy about Jesus. You invited him to church. You were his only friend. What do you think your recent actions have showed him about God or your character? If Jesus had been standing there, would you have called Leroy those names and humiliated him?"

"No, Mom."

"So why did you? God is in you. Your actions show your heart and character. You can't say you are a Christian and act in that way. That is what people call a hypocrite, and that will destroy your character and testimony. You should be standing for what is right and good. Maybe the choice of friends you have made this year is not wise. If you are not influencing others, then they are influencing you. Don't compromise who you are to make 'friends.' Understand?"

He nodded his head and apologized. I then explained that, as a consequence, he would lose his cell phone and all electronics until he proved trustworthy. He also had to write a letter of apology to the boy, his family, and the teachers for his poor behavior.

That night, I had a lot of time to reflect. Why had I been so angry? Why did I lose my head? Why did my son choose to follow the wrong crowd? I am not one of those parents who says, "Not my kid." I'm fully aware that children will make less-than-smart decisions and that they have to learn and grow. Our job is to teach them.

It was then that God dealt with me. Ethan had been wrong for his behavior and deserved consequences for his action, but he did not deserve my initial reaction or words. The Bible says, "Let no corrupting talk come out of your mouths, but only such as is good for building up, as fits the occasion, that it may give grace to those who hear" (Ephesians 4:29). My initial response was from a place of anger. My words were just as sharp to my son's heart as my son's words were to Leroy. Yes, I pulled myself away and regrouped, but I was still wrong.

The following day, after getting the kids ready for school, we prayed before Ethan went to the bus stop. I looked at him and said, "Ethan, I was wrong for how I handled the situation. Please forgive me. I am not perfect. I was angry, and I will try to do better."

"Okay, Mom," he said. "Love you."

When he came home from school that day, he said, "Mom, I wrote to my teachers and said sorry. I asked them to change my seat so I won't be tempted to do the wrong things, and they did. But I didn't write to Leroy. Instead, I went up to his face and said I was so sorry. He said he forgave me, and we sat together at lunch."

Two years have passed since that day, and Ethan is in a better place. Not only are the boys the best of friends, but our families do life together. We need to be careful not to judge ourselves against others or to judge others—and that includes our children. We need to operate in the same grace as God shows us. I had false expectations that Ethan would handle pressure differently, and I allowed rage to control my actions. God dealt with me, and I chose to ask my son for forgiveness, teaching him that Mom's not perfect. He did what was right, and Leroy forgave him, as Ethan forgave me. As a result, two families have become life friends—a true testament to love, forgiveness, and grace.

REFLECTION

Reflect on Ephesians 4:29. Choose your words wisely, for out of the heart, the mouth speaks. Make sure you are not holding on to false expectations that lead to large disappointments. It's in those places we tend to use corrupt words—words that can hurt us or others. Ask God to guide your words daily so you can lead by example.

PRAYER

Heavenly Father, thank you for correction and the ability to learn and grow from our mistakes. I pray that you help us to give our friends, family, and children the same grace you give us when we need to be corrected. Please guide our words that we may not be the source of someone else's pain, and if we are, please bring us to a place of repentance and restoration for all.

In Jesus's name, we pray. Amen.

15

Hero or Villain?

The villain is just a broken hero.

—Mr. J.

After a long, emotional day, in which demands were high, stress was higher, and feelings of inadequacy were even higher, I just wanted the day to be done. I wanted the boys to stop fighting and the house to clean itself. I just needed a break. Movie night was my way out and my chance for quiet and peace of mind. I turned on *Spider-Man 3* and sat with the boys. They were completely engaged, and I had a chance to work on a crochet project without playing referee. As I took a deep breath and enjoyed the relative silence, the words of supervillain Flint Marko got my attention.

In the scene, Flint Marko (the man who killed Spider-Man's uncle) breaks into his old home to see his terminally ill daughter. His ex-wife discovers him, they exchange words, and she kicks him. He says, "I am not a bad person. Just had bad luck." He looks at his daughter and promises to be back with the money to continue her treatment. Later on, he gets stuck in a sand chamber and is blasted with radiation and turns into the famous Sandman.

Throughout the movie, Sandman robs, steals, and destroys in the name of his daughter. The obstacles that try to come up against him cannot slow him down. The heroes or villains who try to take him out single-handedly are not successful. Whenever he is knocked down, his resolve becomes greater. He does all he can and gives all he has for his daughter, even if it means his life. However, the fight is too much. The obstacles he faces slowly wear him down. He loses hope and his source of power. Before his death, he asks Peter Parker to forgive him for killing his uncle.

Flint Marko's quote from the beginning of *Spider-Man 3* echoed through my head: "I am not a bad person. Just had bad luck."

Supervillain or hero? It had me thinking—Flint was human and desperate to do all he could to save his daughter. Desperation, no help, and exhaustion led him to make a series of bad choices in the name of love. He had his hope—and, therefore, his power—attached to something physical (money) instead of eternal. It cost him his marriage, his daughter, and his life. I wonder how many of us have made less-than-perfect choices in life. How many of us have lost our heads for little to nothing, shattering the hearts of our children? How many husbands were in the line of fire of our sharp tongues, purely from our frustration?

I wonder how many of us have hurt friends, family, or coworkers with our words or actions because we were in a bad place. How many of us refused to forgive someone who hurt us from their bad place? My pastor once told me, "Hurt people hurt people," and this supervillain was the perfect example. We can become the villains of our lives without even noticing. If we are not careful with where we place our hope and trust, we can fall into the same trap—taking on the weight of this world alone; trying to be the perfect mom, wife, and friend; always holding ourselves to unrealistic standards—and the pressure will start to break us down, as it did Sandman. We are not meant to be superhumans; we are meant to rely on God's superstrength.

> With man it is impossible, but not with God. For all
> things are possible with God. (Mark 10:27)

After a long, emotional, less-than-perfect day or week, how do we handle life's pressure—like the villain or the hero? Do we rely on God's strength or our own? If we have been operating out of character or have been misunderstood, have we asked for forgiveness, or are we sitting in defeat?

If we surrender our needs to the Lord, he will give us the power and strength to overcome the obstacles life tosses at us. He will give us the ability to forgive and to humble ourselves to ask for forgiveness. He is our source of strength and hope, so keep connected to the power source and avoid the mistakes Sandman made.

REFLECTION

Are you trying to take on the world in your own supermom strength? Are you feeling anxious, overwhelmed, overloaded, and misunderstood? Reflect on Mark 10:27. Are you allowing God into the situation?

PRAYER

Heavenly Father, thank you for the supermom strength you have given us. We pray that you remind us that we are not in this alone; that alone, we can't face the trials this world has set up against us. But with you, all things are possible. Please help us to cast our cares to you, and as you minimize the mountains in our lives, remind us to maximize your greatness so we don't forget who you are and what you have done for us.

In Jesus's name, we pray. Amen.

16

What You See

Click, edit, post, repeat.

In 2001, America faced the devastation of a terrorist attack. That tragic day took 2,997 lives. In 2005, Hurricane Katrina wiped out the lives of 1,833 people and caused over $80 billion worth of damage. Yet through each disaster, we have pulled together as a country and overcome. As of this writing, we are in the middle of a pandemic that has struck our country at its core. This pandemic has claimed millions of lives worldwide, and before it passes, it likely will claim more. Businesses have closed, and schools have closed, forcing parents to homeschool children. We are in quarantine and must follow "social distancing." Life as we know it has radically changed. Streets are empty, and shopping is done virtually and picked up at the curb. Only essential stores (grocery stores and fast food) are open, and they limit the number of people allowed in to ensure there are six feet of space around people. The COVID-19 virus has drastically altered the lives of Americans, striking fear in many. Some of us are out of work, while others are first responders and/or essential employees who risk their lives to make sure their communities are safe.

During this time of uncertainty, I have tried to make life as normal as possible for my children. We do the normal daily routine, homeschool until noon, then do chores, and then play. We build puzzles, play basketball, learn new hobbies, and watch movies. At night, we do our devotion and pray for our family, friends, and nation. I love posting positive pictures on my Facebook page to inspire others in what is a dark time. One day, as I posted an unattractive, sweaty post-workout picture of me (hoping to motivate my friends to get outside and move), I came across a post that made me sad. A gym friend of mine wrote:

> This morning I was having a conversation with a friend about seeing other people's posts on Facebook about how they are killing it with homeschooling and life right now and pictures of all the amazing learning activities they are doing. We were saying how it made us feel inadequate. My real-life goals right now are that I survive the day with my kids still alive and I don't start drinking till five pm.

She then asked her friends to share "real-life pics" of what we were facing, and she posted a pile of unfolded laundry that she had not been able to tend to.

This post hit me hard, mostly because she said she felt inadequate. She, like many other mothers, cares deeply for her children and stops at nothing to give them the desires of their hearts. I could not believe she felt inadequate. It was then I realized that moms still struggle with feeling like we don't measure up. When I think of all the great leaders in the Bible, many of them felt inadequate. Moses was one of them. Called to rescue the Israelites from slavery in Egypt, he had many excuses as to why he could not save his people. The biggest and final excuse was not being qualified for the call.

> But Moses pleaded with the Lord, "O Lord, I'm not very good with words. I never have been, and I'm not now, even though you have spoken to me. I get tongue-tied, and my words get tangled. (Exodus 4:10)

God then asked Moses who had put the words in his mouth; who was responsible for whether people spoke. But Moses still insisted that he was not good enough for the job. At the end, God gave Aaron to

Moses to help him communicate (speak for him) on his journey, and Moses did what he was asked.

Just as Moses didn't feel he measured up as a leader, we can feel the same as parents, especially on social media. We often compare ourselves, "behind the scenes," with the life of someone's highlighted story caption or Facebook post. Then we wonder why we struggle with insecurities.

Truth is, God chose us as the broken vessels we are. We were chosen to do what he created us to do, including being mothers. Only we can love our children the way they need us to love them and meet their needs in the special way we do. God equipped us to carry out the assignment of motherhood in the same way he equipped Moses to save his people. Just like Moses chose to rescue his people, we have to make the conscious decision to trust God in today's culture and media-driven society. We need to run our own races and stop comparing our lives to other people's edited highlights of what they choose to share.

REFLECTION

In what areas do you feel inadequate? Write them down. Are they real concerns or insecurities? Reread Exodus 4:10–13. What is God speaking to you?

PRAYER

Heavenly Father, thank you for your presence when we feel conflicted and full of insecurities. Today, we pray that in times of uncertainty, we will not fall prey to comparing our lives with the more appealing highlights of someone else's life. Lord, remind us to measure our worth in you and your Word. You are the author and perfecter of our faith. You know the beginning from the end and have chosen to bless us with children and family. I pray that you strengthen us where we feel weak and help us to see ourselves the way you do.

In Jesus's name, we pray. Amen.

17

Happily Ever After

*Just because somebody does not love you the
way you want them to doesn't mean that
they don't love you with all they have.*

—UNKNOWN

When I was a young girl, I dreamed of my wedding day. I made a collage of my dream wedding, honeymoon, and house. In my twenties, my dreams of the perfect wedding, family, and home were still active. I had long talks with my then-fiancé about a romantic wedding on the beach, the perfect modest house, and having four children. Not long after our wedding day, I realized marriage was not what I'd imagined, but despite our differences, giving up was not an option. After eight years of failed expectations, however, I felt different. For the first time, I had no fight. I wanted to give up.

Four kids later, with both of us in school and working full time, the stress and distance between us was more than I could handle. One morning, after sending the kids to school, I sat on my front steps and started to cry. "God, I can't do this anymore. This is not what I signed up for. I do it all and get nothing in return—no help, no romance, no support, nothing. This is not a marriage. I am a single mother with a roommate. I want out."

But God said, "You're not a quitter. You need to love him."

"Really, God? Love him? Did you miss the part where I said I already do everything for the man?"

I walked back into my house to call a trusted friend. After about thirty minutes of me crying and pleading my case, she responded, "Love him. Love is an action, not a feeling. Do him one kindness every day. Eventually, your heart will line up with your action."

My mind was blown. That was the last thing I wanted to hear. I was angry, broken, and hurting. I replayed the words of my mom and dad, over and over, in my mind: *Marriage is work. When you stop working at it, it's over.* Then I replayed the advice from my friend.

Desperate and full of uncertainty, I chose to listen to the wisdom in counsel. Samuel did the same when God sent him to find a new king. He was worried he would get killed if Saul found out, and then he had a preconceived expectation of what the new king would look like.

> When they arrived, Samuel saw Eliab and thought, "Surely the Lord's anointed stands here before the Lord."
> But the Lord said to Samuel, "Do not consider his appearance or his height, for I have rejected him. The Lord does not look at the things people look at. People look at the outward appearance, but the Lord looks at the heart." (1 Samuel 16:6–7)

Samuel listened to the Lord, and the right son eventually was brought before him. David, the youngest son of Jesse and the shepherd boy chosen by God to be king.

God warned Samuel to not have expectations of what he thought a king should look like, and because he listened, Israel had a mighty, God-fearing king. Samuel had to keep his eyes on God and his plan. Doing so prevented him from making a devastating mistake.

I had to choose to do the same. On that day six years ago, I wanted God to change my husband. The list was long, and I felt justified in my demands. God's plan, however, was to change me. He wanted me to love the way he loves. He wanted me to keep my eyes fixed on him and his plans, and he wanted me to be obedient.

After fourteen years of marriage, we are closer now than the day we walked down the aisle. God restored our marriage and love, and he freed us from the curse of false expectations. I have never again questioned my husband's love for me.

REFLECTION

What really messes us up in life is the picture in our heads of how life is supposed to be. Are you struggling with false expectations? So many leaders in the Bible struggled too. Read 1 Samuel 16:6–7 (or read the whole chapter), and meditate on the words God spoke to Samuel and the position that he was in. Write down the area where you are struggling, and hold it to God's Word. Take a step back, and choose to trust in God's plan, not your own.

PRAYER

Father God, thank you for being a way-maker. Thank you for always making a way for us, even when we don't see it. Today, we ask that you give us a revelation in your Word that will help us to let go of expectations we should not have—expectations of our spouses, children, families, coworkers, or even other Christians. We pray that you speak to that fear and that it be broken in our lives. Help us to keep our eyes on your plans and to trust in your way, even if we can't yet see it.

In Jesus's name, we pray. Amen.

18

Commit to the Lift

*The task ahead of you is never as great
as the power behind you.*

—BSN

I am an athlete at heart. I love competition, pain, and the outcome of victory. Pushing my body to absolute limits and breaking them is my thrill. But the real challenge is in my mind. On the journey of reclaiming my health, I joined a local CrossFit. I knew they would challenge me. I knew I would be pushed. I knew I would be held accountable, and I needed all of it. What I did not know was how hard it would be, mentally.

My mind tends to quit long before my body will. One night after work, I rushed to the gym, hoping to make it to the 5:15 class. I walked in ten minutes late and had missed the warm-up, so I was not in the right headspace. It was time to lift, and on this night, we were working on a lift known as a "clean." I loaded the bar with weight, hoping to break my personal record (PR) of sixty pounds. I warmed up with fifty-five pounds and started adding weight.

At seventy pounds, I heard a voice behind me say, "You need more weight!"

I turned and saw my coach. "Really? I am not sure I can lift more. I just beat my PR and that was hard."

"You got it up fine," my coach said. "Get more weight."

I loaded the bar with ten more pounds and stood behind it.

Moment of truth—I had to get eighty pounds off the ground, catch it in a squat, and lift it back up to standing position. I planted my feet hip-width apart, got in position, and took a deep breath. The bar came halfway up, and I dropped it. After the third drop, I looked over at my coach, frustrated, and said, "I just can't get the bar up!"

"You can, and you will," she said. "You need to commit to the lift. Do not pick that bar up again until you are fully committed." And she walked away.

With frustration, I gave myself a minute. What did she see in me that I didn't see in myself? I inhaled deeply and took my positions behind the bar.

I heard her from across the gym. "Are you committed?"

I answered her with a full clean at eighty pounds.

I held the position and then dropped the bar. The energy in the room ignited. I was met with high-fives and fist bumps.

The coach walked over, nudged me, and said with a smile, "I told you that you had that, girl."

That was the sweet smell of victory. I beat my PR by twenty pounds. That night I learned a lot about the power of the mind, the power in our words, and in believing in ourselves.

After the third drop, I could have walked away, defeated, but I didn't. Life throws some nasty obstacles at us—from lost loved ones and betrayal to troubled marriages and unruly kids. We may experience an overwhelming amount of pain and frustration, making us want to walk away from the bar of life.

When King David was a boy, he faced the giant, Goliath. But David was in the right headspace. He knew that the power within him was greater than the obstacle in front of him.

> He said to David, "Am I a dog, that you come at me with sticks?" And the Philistine cursed David by his gods. "Come here," he said, "and I'll give your flesh to the birds and the wild animals!"
>
> David said to the Philistine, "You come against me with sword and spear and javelin, but I come

against you in the name of the Lord Almighty, the
God of the armies of Israel, whom you have defied.
This day the Lord will deliver you into my hands, and
I'll strike you down and cut off your head." (1 Samuel
17:43–46)

Big words for a young boy. We know how the story ends—David
gets the victory with a single shot of a stone to the head. David was
committed to the lift! He was committed to making sure that the Lord
was honored and got the victory, saving his people. David made many
mistakes on his journey to being king, but every time he got out of his
own head and was committed to the Lord's way, he was propelled into
greatness.

The obstacles we face as women and moms have no bearing on the
God we serve. We need to remember that the obstacle ahead of us is
not greater than the God within us.

REFLECTION

What are obstacles standing in your way of peace or victory? Take the
time to read all of 1 Samuel 17. It's a good reminder of the obstacles
and giants we face in life. Then hold your giant against God's Word,
and commit to the lift. Lift your hands to God, and surrender your
troubles to him. Don't take it back.

PRAYER

Heavenly Father, thank you for the obstacles. Without them, we would
not have the ability to be overcomers. Today, we ask that you bring
comfort in the place of pain, perseverance to the one ready to quit, and
the endurance to finish the race. Lord, give us the strength to face our
giants and the desire to commit to your will.

In Jesus's name, amen.

❧

SECTION 4

Living with Uncertainty

The most important thing I learned is that soldiers watch what their leaders do. You can give them classes and lecture them forever, but it is your personal example they will follow.

—GENERAL COLIN POWELL

"Mommy, I scared!" The shaky voice of my toddler penetrated my wall of anger and pierced my heart. I took one last look at the spilled chocolate milk all over my floor, dropped the sponge, and gave Killian a hug. Tears streamed down his face, not because he had spilled an entire cup of milk on my freshly mopped floor but because of how I'd responded to the spill.

The image of him shaking, covering his ears, and crying haunted my mind all day. It was the flame that caused the fire of change inside me. That evening, I tucked him in, kissed his face, and said I was sorry to him for the hundredth time.

After he was settled, I continued to clean up the house and prepare for the next morning, but the incident was burning in my mind. *Is my baby afraid of me? What have I become? Why is my anger and frustration out of control? Have I become my mother? I don't want him to live like that.*

There was only one thing left to do. With tears streaming down my face, I called Mom.

After talking to me for an hour, she reminded of me a sentence that echoed through our house, multiple times a week: *Do what I say, not what I do*

She said, "Julie, I was not the perfect mom. But you can do better. Do not make the same mistakes I did. Remember how it made you feel, and do better. Babies are not born with directions attached to their feet. Learn from your mistakes and change them."

My mom was former military intelligence and ran a militant house. She was strong, disciplined, and extremely orderly, and she expected the same from us. Many times, my siblings and I would run through the house, trying to finish our chores (after a lot of procrastination), before Mom walked in the door—we feared her wrath.

I hated it as a child and rebelled against it as a teen. I shut my mom out and responded to her with anger and resentment until about age nineteen. We had moments of closeness that were robbed by my sharp tongue and anger.

As a new mom, I was treading new territory and feared I had become all the things I hated about my mom. I feared that I would lose my son, and he was only three.

Parents are the leaders in the home. As much as we think our kids will do what they are told and not do as we do, we are wrong. Children, like any person, will follow by example. They will do as we do. We need to lead by example. I refused to set up my son to be the man that could tear down his wife and children with his tongue, which meant I should watch mine.

That night I cried out to God: "God, please help me to be a better mom. Help me to hold my tongue and respond better in stressful situations so my son will grow to be a good man and never hate me."

Life can be a long walk through great uncertainty. How we handle the journey is up to us.

19

Wrecked

*The great paradox of parenting is it moves
both in slow motion and fast speed.*

—UNKNOWN

When Spencer was two years old, we noticed that he had all the same behavior patterns as Killian when he was young. My family would point out all the similarities, but I refused to bite. He was perfect. My wheels began to turn as I watched him struggle with basic recall and impulse control. The fight to get dressed or keep clothes on was a daily struggle.

After putting the kids to bed one evening, my husband said to me, "Babe, what are we going to do if Spencer is autistic? He behaves weird and doesn't know he is inappropriate at times. I want him to have a good quality of life."

Feeling defensive, I responded, "I fought for Killian, and he got through when the odds were all stacked against him. We will do the same for Spencer."

But in my head, I was drowning in fear. When Killian was five, we were told he would never graduate high school, that his IQ was too low, and that he did not have the ability to retain information like other children. The medical professional team that diagnosed him continued to list all his shortcomings. That day, I swore to fight for my son. I fought daily for years to make sure that Killian had a chance at life.

I wiped tears from his face when kids cruelly bullied him, went to countless meetings to fight for his academic rights, and wrote endless emails and letters and made phone calls to ensure that educators were adhering to his IEP (Individualized Education Program) to aid in his success. The road was emotional, exhausting, and full of uncertainty and friction.

Would I have to walk it again, staying strong for my child and crying alone at night; wondering how I would navigate him through the cruelty of this world when others didn't understand or refused to see his shortcomings?

When Spencer was four and a half, we sat in the office of a specialist, whose words ricocheted off the walls and pierced my heart.

"As we suspected, Spencer is on the spectrum." The list of familiar traits echoed through the room as I slowly faded away. I felt empty inside. Devastated, I thought, *Why again? Why will he have to face the same cruelty, challenges, and obstacles as his brother? What if I fail him? What if he won't be successful and have a good life? Will he ever be able to live on his own or hold down a job? Will he be wrongly accused of something because of his ignorance?*

My head was spinning out of control. The dreams I had for my son were shattered by a wrecking ball, and I was facing a road of uncertainty. I felt like the breath in my lungs had been removed.

My husband put Spencer in the car and said, "Are you okay?"

Tears rolled down my face. "*No!* Why Spencer? Why again? I don't know if I can watch him struggle like Killian did. It's not fair. What if I fail him?" I got in the car and slammed the door.

As we began to drive, my husband said, "Hey, he will be okay. Killian was, right?"

That was a long week for me. It was a week of mourning and frustration as I screamed out to God. Why did he allow this to happen to another one of my children? The fear I felt for my son seemed endless.

I called my mom yet again for guidance and understanding, and her response was perfect.

"Julie, what happened to trusting your God?" My mom no longer believes in God, so it was "your" God. "How can you have faith if you are consumed by fear. Trust God in the process. Do what you know to do, and God will do the rest."

I was emotionally and physically exhausted from the internal battle, and I finally hit my knees. I always was trying to achieve goals and overcome obstacles. It didn't take long before I was placed in a submission hold by fears and failures.

But there is a way we can walk in peace when we feel completely wrecked inside. The Bible says, "You keep him in perfect peace whose mind is stayed on you because he trusts in you" (Isaiah 26:3).

My first mistake was allowing the report to overwhelm me with the fear of uncertainty. My second mistake was the false expectation that Spencer would be "normal" (whatever that means), and the third mistake was comparing my life with the lives of others. I allowed the pressure of perfection and fear to create stress and wreak havoc in my heart.

There was no having peace in this time. I was angry that God would allow this, and I did not understand why. But after my tantrum—Mom called me out on that—I fixed my eyes upon the Lord. I chose to trust the Lord in this uncertainty. Regardless of what was held up in front of us, I believed that the God before us was stronger. I had to fully trust in him, which is not always easy but is necessary.

We may not understand why the things around us are falling apart, why the pain is greater than we can bear, or why we are drowning fear. But if we choose to keep our minds on the Lord and trust that he knows the beginning and the end; that his way is perfect, even though the circumstance around us may not be; and we choose faith over fear and trust in the Lord, he will fill us with his peace.

REFLECTION

Are you wrecked inside? Are you consumed by worry and fear? Read Isaiah 26:3. What does it look like for you to keep your mind on God in the middle of uncertainty? What do you need to let go of to fully trust in God? Know that the Word of God does not come back empty. We need to choose to apply it to our lives daily, even when we don't feel like it.

Prayer

Heavenly Father, thank you for always being present, even in uncertainty. Though you are not seen, you are not absent, and we can call upon your name in the middle of any storm. Today, we ask that you remove fear, anxiety, frustration, and stress that sets itself up against us in times of uncertainty. Lord, fill us with your peace and presence so we can walk in victory over the circumstance.

In Jesus's name, amen.

20

Where Is God?

Let your faith be bigger than your fears.

—UNKNOWN

A blood-curdling scream jolted me back to reality. Stumbling out of the shower with soap in my eyes, I quickly grabbed my towel and ran to my son's room. I wiped my face and saw Ethan in front of the bedroom door, shaking.

"Ethan, what happened? What's wrong?"

Paralyzed, he said, "Mom, where were you? I called your name and called, but you didn't come? I had a bad dream. I went to get you, but I couldn't see you. Mom, I am scared."

"E, I was in the shower, buddy. It's after ten. I need to get ready for bed too. Your nightlight is on; your music is on. You have no reason to be scared." I gave him a hug and tucked him back in. I handed him a small Armor of God picture that was once on a keychain. He held it in his hand, as he often did when he was scared. Silent tears streamed down his face; he was trying to be brave and would not look at me.

I said, "E, fear is real. We can see it, and we can feel it. But so is God. If we let fear control us, it will stop us from doing things we love. Fear can cripple us, making us afraid of everything and making us feel alone. But the Bible says in 2 Timothy 1:7, 'For God has not given us a spirit of fear, but of power and of love and of a sound mind.' You know what that means?"

"Nope."

"That means you can speak to the fear, and it has to leave because you are a child of God. So all you have to do is call out to God in the same way you yelled for me. He will fill your room with his peace and presence."

I put worship music on softly in the background and sat on his bed, rubbing his head.

"Mom, where is he? I know he is in my heart, but how will he come and make me feel peace when I am scared?"

"Let me show you." And I prayed with him. After praying, I asked, "Do you feel the difference in the room?"

He reached over and squeezed me. With a smile on his face, he said, "Good night, Mom. Love you."

"Love you too, bud. Sleep tight."

As I walked into my room, I couldn't help but wonder why he'd been so panicked. How could he possibly think that I was gone? I had never left them alone. Why would he think that?

Then I heard God say, "But don't you do the same?"

Whoa—my mind was blown.

As moms, we can be so caught up in fear or worry over the what-ifs that we are not in our right minds. Then we become angry and depressed and feel abandoned, all the while yelling the same thing as Ethan did: "*Where are you*, God?"

That night was yet another wake-up call. As I said to Ethan, fear is real; pain is real. But so is our God. If I almost killed myself in running out of the shower at the sound of my son's panicked scream, how much more quickly would God come to us in our time of need?

REFLECTION

Second Timothy 1:7 gets tossed around a lot, but I encourage you to read every word. Compare it to your emotional state right now. Do you have peace? Strength or power? Love? A sound mind? Or are you paralyzed at the doorway of some unspoken fear?

Prayer

Heavenly Father, thank you for revelation. Thank you for always being there, even though we can't always see or feel your presence. Today, we ask that you strengthen us from inside. Help us to remember that your love for us supersedes the love we have for our own children. If we start to lose our minds this week, remind us that you are always around, especially when we feel alone and scared. Thank you for always answering the call of desperation. Lord, please help us to show our children to walk in your peace and love this week. Fill us with your power and presence.

In Jesus's name, amen.

21

Becoming the Profiler

A worried mother does better investigation than the FBI.

—Bebebon

The work experience of a mom—Uber driver, coach, nurse, chef, dry cleaner, teacher, journalist, party planner, event coordinator, housekeeper, stylist, photographer, administrator, spiritual mentor, and (finally) detective.

With a workload like that, it's no wonder why we hit the floor every morning in need of a good dose of caffeine. When the kids where babies, I drank pots of coffee daily to get through the season of no sleep. As they got older, Starbucks in the middle of the day would give me the boost I needed to keep up with the endless demands of motherhood. But if I could manage to get up before the kids, I loved to sit and read my Bible with a hot cup of freshly brewed coffee, soaking up the peace and quiet. I really appreciated those quiet times—times when God could speak to me, and I could reflect on my thoughts before the daily hustle began.

But this morning was different. This morning was one of me suffering pain I had never felt before. I brewed my coffee and sat at my table, my eyes still burning from the night of crying. My head still was spinning from no sleep and late-night fights with my teenager.

Killian was always a good kid—honest to a fault, loved his family, and obeyed all the rules. Then there was a shift. He started missing curfew and coming home later and later—eventually, he didn't come home at all. I spent nights calling and texting and threatening. I would pace the house, lose my head, and break down and cry.

I then became a private investigator. I started stalking his social media and listening to whoever he was speaking with. I tried to reason with him about the friends he was choosing to hang out with, but, he informed me, I had no idea what I was talking about and needed to stop judging his friends. These friends with whom he spent all his time were trouble—drinking, smoking, and partying. I had reason to be concerned, especially because all those things were out of character for Killian, and I did want him to start messing up now.

Yet he chose to put himself in those situations. Endless nights of fighting and grounding him and fighting some more left me feeling exhausted, heartbroken, sick to my stomach, and afraid. All my greatest fears were about to come true. Was everything I had tried to protect my son from going to happen? Would his life, which I fought so hard to give him, be ruined from the stupid decisions he was making at nineteen?

After weeks of this, I was worn down and defeated. I called my mother, crying, hoping for a glimpse of hope. All she had for me was, "You need to calm down. The harder you push the further he goes. He needs to respect the rules of your home, but you can't control who he is with. Or dates. No matter how right you are, he will make his own decisions and learn from his own mistakes. You did, no matter how hard I tried to warn you and guide you."

Not the answer I wanted. I hung up the phone and poured a cup of coffee.

"God, why? Where did I go wrong? How will I keep him from ruining his life? Why won't he go to church or pray with us anymore?"

Tears of pain and failure streamed down my face as I sipped my coffee, and the words *let him go* echoed through my head. "What? No way. I won't stop fighting for him."

But then God said to me, "Is this how I love you? Do I take your choice from you, although I know what is best for you? Do you trust me, or are you trusting in your own limited ability to parent and protect?"

Oh God—I took my last sip of coffee and noticed something written at the bottom of my cup:

> Don't worry about anything; instead, pray about everything. Tell God what you need, and thank him for all he has done. (Philippians 4:6)

I decided to go to the book of Philippians and read the rest.

> "Then you will experience God's peace, which exceeds anything we can understand. His peace will guard your hearts and minds as you live in Christ Jesus." (Philippians 4:7)

Motherhood is full of uncertainty, but the one thing that is constant is our will to love and protect our children. Unfortunately, no matter how many rules and boundaries we put out there, when our kids become old enough to exercise their free will, they are going to do so, and no matter how prepared we think we are, we are not.

That morning, my mom reminded me that I had to learn certain lessons on my own. God reminded me that he was always present in all choices I have made and loved me unconditionally. He also reminded me that I am limited (no matter how good of a PI I am), but he is not. That day, I chose to lift my son up to him and thank him for the man he *will* become.

Each day got better and better. Now, Killian is navigating his life and is coming to me for advice. It is not easy at times, watching him make foolish choices, but God has given me peace, as promised in Philippians.

REFLECTION

Reread Philippians 4:6–7. Hold it up to your situation of uncertainty. Are you being purposeful in your prayer time? Do you trust that God will meet your needs? Are you experiencing his peace? If not, write this scripture down, post it on your fridge, and read it every day, as a reminder to bring your needs to the Father.

Prayer

Thank you for speaking to us through your word. Please help us to remember that we are limited in what we can do, but you are limitless. We pray that pride does not hinder us from bringing our petitions to you. Please steady our hearts, and continue to give us the peace that surpasses all understanding when we are staring into the face of uncertainty.

In Jesus's name, we pray. Amen.

22

Unhinged

Here I am high in surrender I need you now.
—HILLSONG UNITED

One night, after a desperate, soul-wrenching cry to the Lord, I picked up my phone to journal my thoughts. My Bible app sent me a "scripture of the day":

> Consider it pure joy, my brothers and sisters, whenever you face trials of many kinds, because you know that the testing of your faith produces perseverance. Let perseverance finish its work so that you may be mature and complete, not lacking anything. If any of you lacks wisdom, you should ask God, who gives generously to all without finding fault, and it will be given to you. (James 1:2–8)

I remember reading that and saying, "God, really?"

I am super-independent and self-motivated, and I lack patience. I always thanked my Latin roots for the lack of patience and quick temper, but as I grew in faith, I learned how to stifle the fire of frustration before it burned through a room of people, causing damage I couldn't fix or would later regret.

"I need some Jesus before I lose my mind"—that sentence is code to my family for, "Worship on; headphones in; leave me alone."

It was with a song that I learned to combat the fire of frustration, allowing me the time to get clarity and calm down. It seemed to work without fail. No matter the circumstance, when I felt that anger or frustration rising inside of me, I would go to a place of worship. Worship had become my weapon.

But in this season, the song was not enough. My heart was breaking in ways I had never experienced. My chest felt like someone was sitting on it. All I could do was cry.

One evening, after the typical nighttime routine—feed the family; go to the gym—I headed to the church for a meeting. I was a bit late but slipped in the back and listened to the lecture on what was to come for our large outreach. As soon as we were done, I slipped out just as quietly as I'd slipped in, hoping no one would see me.

Then, a woman I love and respect grabbed my shoulder. I turned quickly to see Mrs. Chris smile and hug me.

"Julie, how are you. Really?" her gentle voice said quietly in my ear.

"Walk with me," I replied. On the way to our cars, I begin to break down. "I can't do this. I just can't. If I can't keep one child under control, how am I supposed to raise up the others. My oldest has lost his mind. There is a girl, and I won't allow him to sleep over. He stays out all night, not coming home till four a.m. He is being super-short and disrespectful. He no longer takes care of his responsibilities at home. And when he is home, he fights with me. I cry every night, wondering if he will walk through the door. Yet he blames me for not allowing him to live his life. I can't think straight. I am short with my other kids. My daycare kids are sucking the life out of me. By five p.m., I have nothing left for my family. I can't do this. I am drowning, and God is not listening to my cries. No matter how hard I pray and cry, my prayers are falling on deaf ears. What if I lose Killian and mess up the other three? What am I doing wrong?"

She placed her hand on my shoulder and softly smiled. A peace came over me instantly, and I stopped crying. "Stay strong," she said. "This is a painful season, but you're doing the right thing—teaching him boundaries in a culture that knows none. You will get through this. I went through this with one of my boys. I feared he would end up in jail for all his poor choices. Just like Killian, he was distant and would not listen to anything I had to say. The pain is like no other because we love our children deeply. But remember that God loves us and our children even deeper. Killian is a good kid. He has a good heart, and you raised him right. No matter what you see right now, trust God for the outcome. Praise him in the storm, and never stop praying for your kids."

That night, my soul cried out in desperation, and God answered with the scripture:

> Consider it pure joy, my brothers and sisters, whenever you face trials of many kinds, because you know that the testing of your faith produces perseverance. Let perseverance finish its work so that you may be mature and complete, not lacking anything. If any of you lacks wisdom, you should ask God, who gives generously to all without finding fault, and it will be given to you. (James 1:2–5)

"Really, God? Really?" I asked in frustration. "What kind of joy can I find in the fact that my son is hanging with the wrong crowd? That he chooses to get intimately involved with a girl and stops coming home? What joy can I find in the prospect of becoming a grandmother and him having a child out of wedlock? Where is the joy in watching my child repeat the same mistakes I made when I was young? You want me to find joy in the destruction of my son's future? What am I lacking? What am I missing?"

As I read the words over and over, I realized that what God was saying. This trial with my son was developing something in me. It was stretching me in ways I had never been stretched. It was shaking me at my core. Yet I refused to give up on him, no matter how much it hurt.

But the key was my maturity and what I was missing. Was I handling this fragile season the right way or the way I thought I knew how? Clearly, my hot temper, tongue lashings, and constant scolding was only pushing him further away. I was missing the *wisdom* aspect in this scripture. It was time for me to ask. Every day, I prayed for wisdom, and every night, I prayed for my son and his protection. Each night, I would cry less and began to have peace as I operated in the wisdom that God had given me. Things were not always perfect, but the promise of God is.

REFLECTION

Are we becoming unhinged in the chaos of life? Are we persevering? Or are we lacking in wisdom? Read James 1:2–7. Hold it to the Word of God. How are you reflecting this passage? What are you missing— strength, perseverance, or wisdom? Are you ready to ask God for the wisdom you need to get through this trial?

PRAYER

Heavenly Father, thank you for the gift of wisdom. Today, we pray that you fill each of us with wisdom and peace. Help us to see the circumstances before us through your eyes and that we would not be shaken, no matter how big the giant is. Let us find joy in the middle of the storm, knowing that it will mature us and grow us stronger in faith. We pray that we find strength in your Word and continue to walk in peace over frustration.

    In Jesus's name, we pray. Amen.

23

Borrowed

To raise a child who is comfortable enough to leave you means you have done your job. They are not ours to keep. But to teach how to soar on their own.

—UNKNOWN

The Walt Disney Company has countless family movies that bring us nostalgic feelings of childhood, laughter, and fun. As a child, I compared myself to Ariel, the Little Mermaid, because I felt trapped in a home where Mom did not understand my dreams or who I chose to love. I would sing the songs from the movie, pretending I was Ariel. As an adult, I have watched some of those movies again with my children, and I saw them from a new perspective.

Against her father's wishes, Ariel left the sea because she fell in love with a human. Princess Jasmine left the walls of the palace to escape the overprotected life she lived as a princess. Young Simba could not wait to be king and, against his father's wishes, went into the elephant graveyard. In a recent and modern movie, *The Incredibles*, all three of the children disobeyed their parents by sneaking out to fight crime alongside them. These movies paint the picture of real-life struggles that we face as parents when our children enter into the adolescent and young-adult stages of life. The poet Kahlil Gibran wrote it like this:

> And a woman who held a babe against her bosom
> said, Speak to us of Children.

And he said:

Your children are not your children.

They are the sons and daughters of Life's longing for itself.

They come through you but not from you,

And though they are with you yet they belong not to you.

You may give them your love but not your thoughts,

For they have their own thoughts.

You may house their bodies but not their souls,

For their souls dwell in the house of tomorrow, which you cannot visit, not even in your dreams.

You may strive to be like them, but seek not to make them like you.

For life goes not backward nor tarries with yesterday.

You are the bows from which your children as living arrows are sent forth.

The archer sees the mark upon the path of the infinite, and He bends you with His might that His arrows may go swift and far.

Let your bending in the archer's hand be for gladness;

For even as He loves the arrow that flies, so He loves also the bow that is stable.

This poem, titled "On Children," starts by challenging the very thought pattern of us as parents. "What do you mean they are not *my* children? I gave birth to them. I carried them for nine months. I fed them, clothed them, and loved them. They are my pride and joy. They are my world."

But moms, that the very first mistake we make. We claim them as ours and spend their lives—and ours—swearing that we will allow nothing to ever happen to them. Truth is, they are not ours; they belong to the Lord, and we have them on borrowed time. We are responsible for raising them the best we can, showing them how to be independent, well-rounded, loving, and caring humans. But they are not ours. They have minds of their own, wills of their own, dreams of their own, and goals of their own.

Someday, they will exercise their independence and challenge us in ways we never expected, all to prove they are ready to take on the world and start lives of their own. How do we handle this?

In the book of Luke, Jesus tells us the parable of the Prodigal Son.

> Jesus continued: "There was a man who had two sons. The younger one said to his father, 'Father, give me my share of the estate.' So, he divided his property between them.
>
> Not long after that, the younger son got together all he had, set off for a distant country and there squandered his wealth in wild living. After he had spent everything, there was a severe famine in that whole country, and he began to be in need." (Luke 15:11–14)

The father had two sons. One wanted to test his wings and leave the nest, while the other stayed put. Nowadays, people might refer to them as the good son and the bad seed, meaning that the good son would stay put and do what he was told, making his parents pleased and proud. The bad seed, however, would dare to exercise his own will and rebel against what his parents told him.

In this story, the father divided his portion of inheritance, gave his rebellious son what he asked, and let him go. He did not give his son a laundry list of reasons why he would fail. He did not keep all his inheritance from him and send him out to fail. He did not lecture him on how he would destroy his life by leaving with all his father had built for him.

No, he released him. Day and night, the father looked out in the distance in hope of his son's return. The father never gave up on his son—or should I say, on the Lord. The story continues with the child blowing his inheritance and discovering the ugly realities of having no money, no friends, no food, and no home. The child was allowed to make his mistakes and feel that pain and pressure. It was that pain and pressure that brought him to his senses, and he returned home, where his father ran to him, full of love and compassion and gladness. His son "was lost but now found"—lost in his idealization, lost in his mindset, lost in what he thought was better. But learned the truth out there on his own. He got his share of bumps and bruises and grew from his mistakes. It was a hard lesson for the son to learn. If you read the entire story, you can see his sorrow and pain. A harder lesson for the father, however, was in releasing his son, knowing the pain and hardship that lay ahead of him and that he wouldn't be able to protect his son from it.

My hope is to be like the father—to be the parent who will release my son and trust the Lord for his keeping. If my son returns home after life fails, I hope to be the parent who runs to him with love and compassion, embracing him and choosing to love, despite his past choices. I want to be the parent who always chooses grace and love, trusting in the Lord to protect what I release so my boys will one day fly on their own.

REFLECTION

Read the poem "On Children" by Kahlil Gibran and pull out the truths. God is the archer, we are the bow, and our children are the arrows. Are we trusting the archer to guide the direction of release? Reread Luke 15. Remember that our children will face hardship and pain. We can't protect them from everything, but we can be there to support, encourage, and guide them, allowing God to lead.

PRAYER

Heavenly Father, our children are the most precious gift we have. The love we carry for them is beyond any other in this human realm. But we know your love for us and our children is even deeper, as you created us. Please help us to release our children and allow them to make their own mistakes while they navigate their lives. Please help us to put our complete and total trust in you when we can't see the outcome that lies before our children. We pray that you give us the grace and love to extend to our children, as you do for us.

In Jesus's name, amen.

24

Kneeling When You Can't Stand

When life gets too hard to stand, kneel.
—GORDON B. HINCKLEY

From the day we are born, we face uncertainty. As babies, we cry, waiting for a parent to care for us. As young children, we fear the dark. *What if there is something there? What if Mom or Dad isn't there when I call?* As young children, we fear school. *What if I don't make friends? What if teachers are mean?* As youths, we face more uncertainty. *What if our grades are not enough? What if the boy I love rejects me? What if I don't get into the college I choose? What happens when I move out?* As young adults, we face even more uncertainty. *What if I don't find the one? Will I always be alone?* When we get married, we have other concerns. *Will we have children? Will they be healthy? Can we afford another child? Can we afford that house? What happens if one of us loses a job? Divorce is everywhere—will that be our fate if things get bad?*

In every season of life, we face uncertainty, but when we become moms, that intensifies. From the day we find out we are expecting, everything changes in us. We no longer live our lives for us but for the health and well-being of our babies. When they are born, that instinct to love and protect does not go away and neither does the pain of life from which we try to shelter and protect our children.

But we can't fight fear with fear. We can't expect to live a life of peace and victory if we bow down to every uncertainty that lies ahead of us.

The book of Psalms says, "I will instruct you and teach you in the way you should go; I will counsel you with my eye upon you" (Psalm 32:8).

For us to receive instruction or counsel, we need to be in a position to hear it, accept it, and receive it. If we are busy asking our friends, family, spouses, or mentors for counsel, then when do we have the time to hear the instruction of the Lord? It's not wrong to share your pain with loved ones. It's not wrong to seek counsel from a mentor in your life. However, God wants us to depend fully on him and allow him to be the one to sustain us and guide us.

A few years back, when I was going through some trials and stepping down from ministry positions, I felt so lost, alone, and overwhelmed by grief that I found myself belting out the lyrics to one of Kari Jobe's songs. It was a reminder that even though I was broken and had nothing left in me, I trusted that God would meet me in the mess—the key word being *trusted*. I didn't *feel like* he would; I *trusted* he would. With tears streaming down my face, I choked out the words:

> When my hope is gone
> When the fear is strong
> When the pain is real
> When it's hard to heal
>
> When my faith is shaken
> And my heart is broken
> And my joy is stolen
> God, I know that you lift me up
>
> —Kari Jobe, "Find You on My Knees"

After listening to it, over and over and over again, something happened in me. The tears would not stop coming, and I took the position that God had been waiting for. I was at the end of myself and hit my knees. Finally, I was in a place to hear, accept, and receive what the Lord was saying to me. In order for the Lord to instruct and counsel us, we must be willing to go to him. Let's be the women who go to our knees before our loved ones so we can grow in what God has for us, in good times and in troubled times.

REFLECTIONS

Are you drowning in fears of the unknown? Have you come to the end of yourself? Are you ready to allow God to instruct your direction? Read Psalm 32:8. What will stop you from receiving instruction from God?

PRAYER

Father, we thank you so much for the stretch. It is a painful process and full of uncertainty, but in the stretch, we develop flexibility and strength. We pray as we face uncertainty, pain, or even areas where we feel we are being stretched beyond what we can handle. We pray that we become the women who hit our knees first and wait for your counsel. We ask as we wait that you fill us with your peace. May we develop a more intimate closeness with you that draws others to desire you deeper.

In Jesus's name, we pray. Amen.

SECTION 5

Intimacy Interrupted

"He wasn't exactly sure when it had happened. ...All he knew for sure was that right here and now, he was falling hard for this woman, and he could only pray that she was feeling the same way."

—Nicholas Sparks[3]

I was twenty-five when I sat in my mother's living room, crying, after putting Killian to sleep one evening. "Will I ever fall in love again? Will I ever be married? I can't picture myself with anyone else."

"Julie, you can't see it now, but the right person will come," my mom said. "And he will love both you and Killian. When that happens your love for Kilian's father will be a distant memory. Your heart will belong to someone else."

A few short months later, I met a man. We had a lot of fun together. He made me laugh; he made Killian laugh; and, without warning, he stole my heart. Love is a funny thing. It is embracing the slow climb

---

[3] Nicholas Sparks, *Safe Haven* (New York: Grand Central Publishing, 2017), 117.

and quick fall of a roller-coaster ride. You see potential in what could be, to the sudden drop of losing control of your heart and all that you thought was rational.

Without warning, a friendship turned into a romance, and that romance lit a fire so deep in my soul that I couldn't picture a life without him. Sure enough, my mother was right—my heart now belonged to someone else. However, "A priceless moment is when the person that you have fallen in love with looks you right in the eyes to tells you that they have fallen in love with you" (the Coach, raiseyourmind.com).

The night he told me that he loved me was the start to our forever journey.

25

Vows

So, it's not going to be easy. It's going to be really hard; we're going to have to work at this every day, but I want to do that because I want you. I want all of you, forever, every day. You and me ... every day.

—Nicholas Sparks[4]

Just like any other love story, our love story is unique. We met online on a dating site. I played hard to get for a few weeks, but he was persistent. We started dating, and after a few short months, we were head over heels in love. We had dreams of a life together—building a family and making a home. We talked about growing old together and enjoying our children and grandchildren. We knew we wanted to spend forever together, and forever could not start soon enough.

After speaking to our then-pastor, Matt and I started marriage counseling, and six months from the day we started dating, we were married. Lots of people had lots to say about our decision to get married so quickly, but for us, it felt right. We "knew" it would be work, but we were ready to take the next step.

Part of our vows was 1 Corinthians 13:4–5: "Love is patient, love is kind. It does not envy, it does not boast, it is not proud. It does not

---

[4] Nicholas Sparks, *The Notebook* (New York: Grand Central Publishing, 2016), page number.

dishonor others, it is not self-seeking, it is not easily angered, it keeps no record of wrongs."

Oh, how romantic. Love is so wonderful; it's everything I want in a marriage. This is the best day of my life.

Shortly after the vows, reality hit. All those things people told us about marriage being work started to make sense. Things around us were definitely not all roses and sunshine, but at the end of the day, we still wanted each other.

I always thought love was a feeling. People fall in love and, based on my past experience, out of love. I never wanted that to be true for me. I did not want to have a failed marriage, so, like any other overachiever, I started to research how to make my love for my husband last throughout time.

Our culture has a very different view on keeping a man around. Society has painted an image of the hot housewife, always being available sexually, while maintaining a family, a house, and her appearance. If we keep our youthful, before-children body and don't lose our sex appeal while maintaining family life, then our spouses won't need to look somewhere else. At least, that is what our culture says.

While that may hold some truth, it is not how God designed us. Men and women become one. That unity should be sacred and requires attention to keep it healthy and growing, like any living thing. Sex appeal is conditional and won't last forever, so rooting your relationship in something so shallow is like building on sinking sand.

One year, I hosted a small group discussion in my home. The topic was "Verbs of God." In this time, God revealed to me his active love for us, even when we don't see him. Love is an action, not a feeling. The feeling is just the by-product of the action.

This realization changed what 1 Corinthians 13:4–5 meant to me.

Now I realize that it is the direction to a successful marriage. It is a measuring stick of my actions to my spouse. Was I being patient? Was I being kind? Was I being self-seeking or holding records of wrong?

Self-examination is never fun, but it's necessary. As the circumstances around us change, our lives change, and we change. Part of this process is looking inward and taking responsibility where we fall short.

If we fail to do this, we allow our changing desires to slowly sneak in to our marriages, creating small, harmless indifferences. Then, someday, those harmless indifferences become a great division because we did not address them.

Love is a verb.

Work is a verb.

We need to take action and be vigilant, guarding our hearts and protecting the gift God gave us first—marriage.

REFLECTION

This can be a painful but necessary reflection. Have you taken the time to self-examine the kind of spouse you are? Where do you and your spouse have the most disagreements? How do *you* respond to the situation (without pointing at his action that "caused" your response)? Take that situation and your response, and hold it to 1 Corinthians 13:4–5. Does your response line up with the scripture? If not, where do you fall short? Take that, and work on it this week. If it's patience, try to take a deep breath and regroup before talking. If it's kindness, show *acts* of kindness, even if you don't feel like it. Serve him coffee, or give him extra attention. If what you feel like saying is dishonoring, hold your tongue. Whatever God has revealed to you, take action in correcting it, and allow God to correct your spouse.

PRAYER

Heavenly Father, thank you for the gift of love. Thank you that you died for us, showing us the ultimate love sacrifice. We pray that, today, we never forget that love is a choice. It is an action, and you have reminded us of this throughout scripture. Please help us to remember this when life hits, and we feel surrounded by chaos. Please illuminate the areas we need to work on in showing more love to our spouses and children, and as we take action, may their hearts do the same.

In Jesus's name, we pray. Amen.

26

Then There Were Six

*I am just a mom standing in front of her husband,
trying to say something that I can no longer remember
because our kids have interrupted us 175 times.*

—MOMMY OWL

After a year of marriage, Matt and I decided it was time to expand our family and give Killian a sibling, but growing a family was a process we did not expect. Getting pregnant should have been easy, but it wasn't for me. Pregnancy should have been a joyful time, but it was full of complications and pain. Delivery is usually full of anticipation and excitement, but ours was full of uncertainty, as I went under the knife, unable to deliver naturally. All of our children were planned, and each of them had a unique set of problems. Yet each time we got pregnant, we hoped we would experience the "normal" sleep-deprivation new moms experience—the normal late-night cries and feedings that eventually go away. But for the first year of each of our boys' lives, we faced long days and endless nights of screaming kids, with little to no reprieve. With colic, acid reflux, and lactose intolerance, our infants were a handful. It's no wonder that having more children changed the dynamic of our relationship and our home.

The only way to have quiet and get things done was to carry them against my chest in their MOBY Wrap. At that point, I felt like Doc Ock, managing all things around me like I had multiple arms. From helping with schoolwork, to keeping up with house chores and cooking dinner, to ministry responsibilities, I had learned to manage life with a child attached. I did everything in my power to keep my sanity and their comfort. Every night, I would fall asleep with a baby in my arms, propped up in bed so I could rest. This left little time for my husband. I was too tired to meet his needs or even talk with him. I would justify this by saying, "This season will pass."

But as the children got older, I focused more on their growing needs, putting them first, above my marriage. After all, that's what a good mom would do, right?

I once worked a marriage retreat for my pastor's mentor. I watched as the room filled with couples, all striving for the same thing—creating more intimacy in their marriage. I thought my marriage was fine—until the pastor and his wife started hitting on some topics that kill intimacy in marriage. One was sex. He referred to it as "homework." Are we meeting the emotional and sexual needs of one another? Are we talking about where we fall short in the marriage bed? Are we learning from each other?

The other was children. Children are a gift from God, but your husband comes before children. (Yeah, okay.) When I was a single mom for five years, my son always came first, and it was not about to change. I did not understand how a grown man's needs should come before my child. After a couple of years, however, I no longer recognized my husband, and the strain on our marriage was evident. We had become strangers.

One night, during my internship with Dr. Joel Johnson, we were discussing the five essentials to a healthy marriage. Dr. Johnson explained to us that healthy marriage is intentional. We need to be intentional about our time with our spouse. We should schedule time in our calendar weekly to connect. If we don't, there will always be something that consumes all our time. This was especially true for our children.

Then he said something that struck a chord: "We should love and adore children but not above spouse." Clearly, I was missing something. I decided to search scripture to see if this was actually true. Out of all the scripture I read, this was the one that hit the hardest:

"Have you not read that he who created them from the beginning made them male and female, and said, 'Therefore a man shall leave his father and his mother and hold fast to his wife, and the two shall become one flesh'? So they are no longer two but one flesh. What therefore God has joined together, let not man separate." (Matthew 19:4–6)

There it was—part of our vows again. Matt had left his mother to become one with me, forever my companion, and me his. That's what we wanted when we said *I do*. But here it is the sentence: "What therefore what God has joined together let no man separate," and my eyes were open. *No man*—that includes our kids—should separate our marriages. I had failed my husband. We were strangers because I chose to put our children before our marriage.

Not only was that advice sound, but it also changed the course of our marriage. I can happily say that we are more in love now than the day we said *I do*.

REFLECTION

Are areas in your marriage suffering? What does that look like? Be honest, and write down the things that seem to be broken in the marriage. Reflect on Matthew 19:4–6. As you reflect on that passage, think about how you can communicate your concerns to your spouse. Communication kills confusion. Confusion causes division. Let's not allow confusion to divide our homes. Take some time to pray and reflect on this. If you need help in communicating your concerns, I encourage you to seek counsel from your pastor.

PRAYER

Lord, thank you for the gift of marriage. Thank you for our forever friends and companions. Lord, we ask that you help us see where we fall short, and give us the words to communicate effectively with our spouses. This is not easy, but we pray that we use our two ears to listen and our one mouth to speak. Communication without understanding is just talk, so please help us to take the time to hear our spouses' concerns and grow closer together. Let nothing and no man separate what you have brought together.

In Jesus's name, we pray. Amen.

27

Comfort Zone

Change is inevitable; growth is optional.
—John Maxwell

I remember a time when I had more shoes than my closet could hold—shoes to match accessories and outfits. I had what inner-city folk called "shoe game." I also remember when my hair and makeup was always on point. I remember when my accessories matched my shoes, and I had an ungodly amount of jewelry to choose from every morning. It was normal for me to wake up ninety minutes before I had to be anywhere so I could have enough time to get ready. My image was important to me. It didn't matter if I was going to the gas station or to the store. I always wanted to feel like I was turning heads and snapping necks. When I got pregnant, women would tell me, "Don't let yourself go after you give birth. It happens to the best of us." I didn't know what they were talking about. How could someone be satisfied with looking frumpy? I swore that would not be me.

Fast-forward a year, and I was swallowing my words. Because I was unable to fit in my prebaby clothes, I got depressed and ate my emotions (as if that was helpful). After years of yo-yo dieting, I gave up and settled for my new normal. I justified it by saying that my budget as a single mom was tight, when really, I'd stopped caring and got comfortable with the convenience of not spending an hour on my appearance.

One day, while visiting with my parents, my mom said with disapproval, "How do you expect to find a husband looking like that?

What happened to you? You're young and beautiful. If you would just take care of yourself, any man would want you."

My response to that was—let's just say it was nothing nice. If someone wanted to marry me, he should want me for who I was, not just my looks. But after self-examination, again I had to make changes. Proverbs 1:32 states, "For simpletons turn away from me—to death. Fools are destroyed by their own complacency."

Complacency is a quick and silent killer of passion and love. Once we feel we have reached success or can't go further, we can become idle. Stuck in mediocrity, we stop growing or bettering ourselves. We trap ourselves in toxic relationships, with complacency allowing our passions to die and our indifference to grow. This holds especially true in our relationships with God and our spouses.

Can you imagine if God had allowed himself to be complacent? Can you imagine what this world would look like? The amount of pain and tragedy our nation sees would be much worse. So thank God that he hasn't become complacent and never will.

We were made in God's image. Our marriages are a reflection of Christ's love for his people. I saw it written like this:

> Marriage is not "Do unto others as they have done
> unto you." It is actually "Do unto others as Christ
> has done unto you." (Bradley and Amanda Bennett,
> The Us Equation)

Now that's a picture to reflect on. It brings me back to Corinthians 13. Throughout the gospel, we see God's undying love for his people, regardless of the situation. He has never quit or gotten lazy in his pursuit of loving us. But unfortunately, we are different. We allow pain and disappointment to misguide us right into the trap of complacency. From our walk with God to our relationships with our spouses, we begin to unravel into depression and self-destruct—and then wonder why. The answer is easy. Complacency is our own self-satisfaction with where we are and being oblivious to the danger signs around us. It is the opposite of humility. With humility, we self-examine, facing the discomfort it brings and are willing to make changes so we grow in life's challenges.

There is no place for self-satisfaction in a marriage. Marriage is work. We should always be looking into our marriage and seeing where we can improve and grow. Part of that is working on ourselves daily. Are we growing spiritually, mentally, and physically? If not, we are in the danger zone. If we want to give our best to our families, we must never stop growing. Only then will they have our best. If not, complacency will quickly rob our marriages of intimacy because we have become comfortable with going through the motions and routine of life.

Try to keep the passion alive. Never stop pursuing the love of God and your spouse, like you did when you first fell in love.

REFLECTION

Are there areas in your life where you are settling or may be satisfied with not seeing the warning signs around you? In what areas are you flirting with complacency? Is your marriage one of those places? Take time to write down those areas and reflect on Proverbs 1:32.

In those places, do you see the danger signs of self-destruction? Will it cause you to lose yourself or the ones you love? What steps do you need to take to change that?

PRAYER

Father, we want to thank you for never giving up on loving us. Thank you for your endless pursuit, even when we don't deserve it. Thank you for showing us what love is and how we should model it. Today, we pray that you penetrate the walls of our hearts and help us to break free from the areas of our lives in which we may be complacent. We pray that you breathe a fresh fire in our hearts and reignite the passion for the chase. Light a fire in our souls, that we may never stop pursuing you and never stop pursuing our husbands. We pray that you strengthen our marriages and homes.

In Jesus's name, amen.

28

Sex, Love, and Marriage

Great sex does not prove whether a married couple is still in love. Their choosing to love each other unconditionally every day is proof that they are still in love.

—Aaron and Jennifer Smith

Sex is a fun yet taboo topic to talk about, so I guess I'll just jump right in. In our earlier years of marriage, I used to say that I had the libido of a fifteen-year-old boy. I had this unquenchable thirst to have sex and expected Matt to reciprocate. If he did not, I felt rejected and unloved. In my mind, I was giving him the best part of me, and he was rejecting it, so he must not love me. Naturally, I returned the favor when he came looking for a little skin-to-skin, hoping he would feel the sting of rejection. I didn't realize that my perspective of sex and love was slowly poisoning my marriage and would have great consequences.

After years of this game, we started having trouble on the home front. Communication suffered, sex was a "duty," and being a wife was another job to check off the list.

We sought our pastor for counsel, and he pointed out, using scripture, that my actions were wrong.

> The husband should fulfill his marital duty to his wife, and likewise the wife to her husband. The wife does not have authority over her own body but yields it to her husband. In the same way, the husband does

not have authority over his own body but yields it to
his wife. (1 Corinthians 7:3–4)

The scripture clearly says I should not be holding out on my husband. You probably can picture my response. I shot a look at our pastor with great disapproval, and the words that came out of my mouth went something like this: "I am not anyone's sex toy. I refuse to 'put out' because I have to. I have a choice. It's my body, and I refuse to feel forced to have sex if I don't want to. There is not a person in this godforsaken world that can make me. It's my body and my choice."

That counseling session did not end well. Heated and completely annoyed, I went home and refused to acknowledge what our pastor had said. After all, my husband was the one who had pushed me away, so why cry about it? Days and weeks went by, and I still remained cold and indifferent in the marriage bed. I was tired; I had a headache; I had my period—anything to keep him away.

But one late evening, when I could not sleep, I tuned in to the Hillsong Channel (a Christian-based TV network) and was intrigued by a show called *Sex, Love and Relationships*, hosted by John and Helen Burns. They had years of experience and presented unconventional topics. I was interested in their opinion on my problem, and this particular episode touched upon the script our pastor had pointed out—but with a different spin.

"The husband should fulfill his marital duties to his wife, and likewise, the wife to her husband."

My ears were open. What did that look like, and what did it have to do with sex?

As they explained, John came to realize that as Helen was raising the kids and tending to the house, along with ministry obligations, she would grow tired. The chance of his getting sex was slim to none. He figured out what that scripture meant: *help his wife*. I died laughing—but there was some truth to that.

He explained that when he made himself available to help with household chores, it took some stress off Helen, and she made herself physically available to her husband. It was the act of serving that showed her love, not the act of sex. Putting your spouse's needs before yourself is love in action. It can be as simple as late-night talks, helping in the home, or his watching the kids so you can shower.

All of a sudden, the scripture made sense to me. I had been looking at love all wrong and holding back a form of intimacy as punishment. Love is an action, and sex is an expression of the love you already have for one another. Holding out will only cause division in what God meant to be one.

If you're struggling in this area, try meeting the needs of your spouse in another way, creating stepping stones in the ladder of intimacy.

REFLECTION

Is the marriage bed suffering? Take some time to reflect on 1 Corinthians 7:3–4. Are you fulfilling your marital duties? Do you and your spouse have agreements on how you can help each other so you have fewer disagreements? Does your spouse know how he can help you and show you love through other actions outside the bed? If not, it's time for you to have that conversation.

PRAYER

Father, we thank you for the gift of marriage. Today, we ask you to reveal to us how we can show love in action to our spouses, outside of the bed. We pray as those needs are met that you fill us with new passion to meet the physical needs of our spouses in the marriage bed. As we continue to work on our marriages, may our relationships with our spouses grow deeper and stronger.

In Jesus's name, amen.

29

Mental Shift

Whether it's clear to you or not, God is in control. Submit to that, and you will soon see that all is unfolding as it should.

—UNKNOWN

When I was growing up, my mother described me as stubborn, hard-headed, obnoxious, strong-willed, and hateful. It's no wonder she and I never got along. We fought often, and I never understood why my mother "hated me." Naturally, I returned the favor by making her life miserable. (I wonder where I got my strong will? Thanks, Mom.)

As I got older, my will grew stronger, and so did my pride. I always strived to be the best at whatever I was doing, and my way was always the right way.

When my son Spencer was eighteen months old, I started working in full-time ministry. I remember the interview process clearly. My pastor asked to see me, so I went in for a meeting. He asked me if I wanted a job.

I said, "For you? At the church?"

"Yes. I am looking for an admin, and I felt the Lord say you were the one."

I looked at him with disbelief. "Ugh," I said. "Let me pray on it."

We set up another meeting, at which we went back and forth on whether I was "ministry material." I tried for days to convince him that I was not adequate for the job, my temper being the biggest problem. But he was confident that the Lord wanted me there.

I took the position, and within a year in ministry, my will was rocked, and my pride was tested daily. I had to learn to play nice in the sandbox and actually listen and care about other people's perspectives. I would ask God daily, "Are you sure I am right for this position?"

Looking back, I realized God was teaching me submission and growing me in character. According to *Webster's Dictionary*, to *submit* is to "accept or yield to a superior force or to the authority or will of another person."

Working at the church forced me to learn kingdom principles—such as, our pastor is our shepherd; therefore, we submit under his authority and follow him as he follows Christ. Challenging him was not acceptable or tolerated (as I quickly learned).

Years later, I had grown tremendously but still struggled with my temper. One morning, I walked into the pastor's office and said, "Boss, do you have a minute?"

"Of course," he said. "Have a seat."

"I can't do this anymore. I need direction. Why can't I control my temper? My husband and I keep fighting, and he refuses to understand my perspective."

He looked at me and said, "First of all, self-control is a fruit of the spirit. You know when you're going to lose it. Instead of feeding into the anger, start exercising self-control. God lives in you, does he not? Second, you are tearing down the walls of the home you both built with strife. Do you know why?"

I stayed silent, but my face said, *Please do enlighten me.*

"It's because you don't know your place as a wife."

This time, my face said, *Um, excuse me?*

"Julie, you are not the head of your home. Matt is, and God ordained that. Your husband is your covering, and you need to find your place under his authority. Follow him, as he follows the Lord."

I walked out of the office, annoyed. *Know my place?* I thought. *You're kidding, right? Give my authority to my husband? Why? So he can lord it over me? No, thank you.*

Sunday mornings would come, and I was great at putting on a smile and playing "the part"—you know, the Christian who had it all together. After all, I was on staff and lead ministry; we couldn't show we had problems.

"Good morning ... God bless ... How are you?" Blah, blah, blah. But right before I walked in the doors of the church, I had torn off my husband's head and eaten my children alive.

I was sick of feeling like a hypocrite and sick of the fighting. I prayed harder and researched my Word more. I stumbled across this scripture:

> The wise woman builds her house, but with her own hands the foolish one tears hers down. Whoever fears the Lord walks uprightly, but those who despise him are devious in their ways. A fool's mouth lashes out with pride, but the lips of the wise protect them. (Proverbs 14:1–3)

That was it; I was wrecked. My pastor had mentioned I was tearing down my home with strife. The scripture said that with her own hands, the foolish tears down her home. I knew what the Bible said, yet I was being foolish because of my pride—because I was afraid that submitting to my husband meant losing myself and my free will. But it was exactly the opposite.

That night, I asked the Lord to forgive me for choosing the way of the fool and allowing strife to rule my home. Then the mental shift happened. As I began to align myself next to my husband, instead of in front of him, our marriage started getting stronger. I learned that allowing him to lead our home did not mean I was subject to a dictatorship and had no rights. It meant I would honor and respect him as my husband, the provider and protector of our home. It meant I would align myself with God's Word and allow my husband to do as God commanded him—love us, provide for us, and lead us. It meant I trusted God to lead our union and make us stronger as a couple.

How do I do that? I bring my husband honor by backing him up when he corrects our children, even if I feel he was wrong—that gets discussed in private. It means that the more I respect and honor my husband, not tearing him down with words, the more he feels loved and the deeper the bond gets. Believe it or not, not long after I chose to honor my husband, the deeper our love naturally formed. This is a true reflection of how Christ loves his church. It won't always be perfect, but it can and should be done.

REFLECTION

Reflect on Proverbs 14:1–3. Ask if you are being the foolish woman or if you are walking upright with the Lord. Do you have a great hate for the word *submit*? What is the root of that feeling? Write it down. Is it fear of losing yourself? Is it fear of your spouse abusing his authority? Is it pride? Write these things down and bring them to the Lord.

PRAYER

Heavenly Father, today we ask that you help us to walk upright with you, according to your Word. We pray that you give us the trust we need to submit to our spouses, as we submit to your authority. Please help us to see where fear or pride is hindering our ability to align ourselves with your Word. Please forgive us where we have fallen short, and help us to offer the same forgiveness to our spouses.

In Jesus's name, we pray. Amen.

30

Fight

*Ultimately, we need to decide for ourselves
what constitutes failure, but the world is quite
eager to give a set of criteria if you let it.*

—J. K. ROWLING

When I was five, my mom married the man I call Dad. He raised me and my siblings, loving us like we were his own. My mom, hands down, was the disciplinarian, but my dad was the one who came to our rooms to wipe our tears and tell us we were loved. He took the time to bring us out for ice cream to put smiles on our faces.

We had a home of food fights, hide-and-seek, playing in the rain, and laughter. We were (and still are) lucky to have such an incredible dad. Even though we were not biologically his, he loved us as if we were. I never understood what that looked like until I had a son out of wedlock. I prayed and hoped to find a husband like my dad, one who would love me deeply and love my son. A man who committed to me would have to be just as committed to my son.

I thank God for men like my dad and my husband. The impact and influence they have on the life of a child who is not biologically theirs is incredible and noble. They made the choice to commit to what society would call a "premade family" and to love us. As I will say over and over in this chapter, love is an action and requires a lot of work.

Whether you are a blended family or not, marriage still requires work. Part of what is stated in many marriage vows is, "A three-strand cord is not easily broken." A single cord can snap with a good pull, if your strong enough. Two strands are a little harder to snap, but three—that takes scissors.

Our marriages, as Christians, have Christ as the third strand. When trouble hits, we often fail to remember that. When trouble hits, we can easily point fingers at each other, causing more division, instead of connecting with the one who brought us together.

John 16:33 says, "I have told you these things, so that in me you may have peace. In this world you will have trouble. But take heart! I have overcome the world."

I know that's not a typical marriage verse, but I love it because it's a reminder that in this life, in this world, we will have trouble—it's inevitable and to be expected. How we handle trouble in our marriages makes a difference. It's the difference between growing together or apart. It influences and shapes the minds of our children, even if we don't think they are paying attention (they are). It is the difference between walking in peace or in strife.

The troubles we will face as married couples will cause an immense amount of stress, but scripture says to "take heart! I have overcome the world." According to the *Collins English Dictionary*, *take heart* means to have more courage or confidence; cheer up. God asks us to not lose courage. He has overcome this world. In other words, God is still in control in every situation, even during troubled times. Don't lose hope or faith. Trust in the Lord when you can't see through the pain.

Warren Barfield wrote the song "Love Is Not a Fight" for his wife in the middle of their fractured marriage. The lyrics speak so much truth, but the chorus is my favorite:

> Love is a shelter in a raging storm
> Love is peace in the middle of a war
> If we try to leave may God send angels to guard the door
> No, love is not a fight but it's something worth fighting for

When things get shaken and our marriages seem to be unraveling, when our children are unruly and life is full of uncertainty, let's be the people who don't lose their courage. Let's trust God to restore what is broken and start fighting for our marriages. If we turned the tables and stopped fighting in our marriages and started fighting for them, we would show our children important lessons. We'd show them reliance and strength and what it looks like to surrender our marriages to the Lord. We'd show them that love is an action, not a feeling. We'd show our children that if God is in our marriages, quitting is not an option, regardless of what society tells them. We'd show our children what marriage looks like between Christ and his church.

Let's be the mothers who show their kids that society does not define the success of our marriages; God does.

REFLECTION

Reflect on John 16:33. Do you have peace in your marriage? In your life? If you are struggling and feel that there is no hope, write down those places where you're struggling. Then, remember that God asked you to not to lose courage. Can those places be reconciled on your knees before the Lord alone? If not, I encourage you to seek counsel from your pastor, and continue to fight for your marriage.

PRAYER

Thank you, Lord, for always being present and for coming to our rescue in times of trouble. Thank you for the gift of marriage and family. Today, we pray that you restore all that may be broken in the marriages of the women who are reading this book. Please restore hope and passion. Please restore intimacy and communication. Please bring unity to their homes and strengthen their love for one another.

In Jesus's name, we pray. Amen.

Doing Life

*You're not just another person; you're
the love of my life.—God*

—UNKNOWN

Motherhood is multidimensional. There are many facets to the word *mom*. It includes being a good wife, a good mother, a good friend, a good daughter, and—somewhere in there—good to ourselves. It is a twenty-four/seven job and can be both chaotic and messy.

We have times of great happiness and times when we feel great isolation. Some of us may have chosen to take a less-than-perfect path to figure life out on our own.

If this is you, and you are struggling with trying to balance the demands of life and motherhood; if you have chosen to do life your way, hoping for a different outcome, but seem to be falling short, it's time to change. If you're ready to trust God with your life, your children's lives, and your marriage, I want you to pray the following prayer:

Father in heaven,

I am sorry I have fallen short. Forgive me for not trusting you and walking away. Please fill me with your Spirit and help me to walk in line with your Word. I ask you to fill my heart, home, and marriage with your love and presence.

In Jesus's name, I pray. Amen.

About the Author

Julie Whitley is a wife and highly driven, nonstop mother of four boys. She knows the realities of being a mom at every stage of development. She is not afraid to tell it like it is while reminding every mother there is no greater gift than love.